Little by little,
a little becomes a lot.
(African Proverb)

Little by Little

Kilimanjaro

Kerry McGlynn

Little by Little, Kilimanjaro
Copyright © 2024 Kerry McGlynn
All rights reserved.

Books may be purchased at www.KerryMcGlynn.com,
your favorite book seller, or online.

Editing: Sarah Chauncey
Cover and Interior Design: Rebecca Finkel, F+P Graphic Design, FPGD.com

ISBN paperback: 979-8-9910851-0-6
ISBN eBook: 979-8-9910851-1-3

LCCN: 2024916860

Printed in USA

Cover photo: Guide Frederick offering a hand to Craig on the Barranco Wall.

Dear Alison and Craig,

This was written for you.

I love you.

Just the way you are.

Contents

CHAPTER 1

Despair

Sunday, January 19, 2020

Headlamps on, we're just walking in the dark, single-file, up the face of the mountain, hoping to achieve the 19,341 foot summit before altitude sickness forces us to turn around. Although I've worked hard to get here, it is the last place I wish to be right now. I want to quit. I want to go back.

In a few hours, my son and I will be summiting Africa's highest mountain. Unattached to a mountain range, Kilimanjaro is also known as the world's highest freestanding mountain, a majestic monolith rising out of the plains of Tanzania three and a half miles into the sky. For days now, Craig and I have been making the long trek to this highest point of the African continent with the support of a hard-working crew and three other trekkers. Our day today started at sunrise yesterday. These two days have blended into one because of lack of what you would call significant sleep, the measure normally used to separate one day from another. Starting out on Saturday, we had trekked all morning and arrived at our highest camp. Later, after an early dinner, we had been instructed to go to bed for a few hours to rest up before a midnight start for the summit segment.

Craig had been the first one to mention Kilimanjaro. Back in 2012, when he was still in high school, he and I had hiked the Inca Trail, up and over the ridges of the Andes Mountains on the way to Machu Picchu.

"Mom," he said, "I want to do Kilimanjaro someday."

"You want to do what?"

"Mike said he and his family did it last year and that this Inca Trail is nothing compared to that." Mike, an older teen, and his family were trekking the IT with us. "They climbed this really big mountain."

"Oh," I said.

"It's supposed to be a lot more challenging," he said.

Not that I needed anything more challenging. At the time, we lived near sea level in Texas and the highest point on our Andes trek was 13,828 feet at Dead Woman's Pass, a crazy high altitude for us. I didn't know what Kilimanjaro was, or where, but the seed got planted and it became a recurring conversation over the years.

Now, we're on Kilimanjaro. It's a crystal cold night and I'm struggling with altitude, as well as attitude. We've spent the last week with another family, working our way up the mountain, and tonight's summit push began from Barafu Camp at 15,360 feet. A few hours ago our alarm roused us at 11:00 at night and I struggled through the awful haze of inadequate sleep to get dressed. In addition to the multiple layers of clothing I'd slept in, I put on a sturdy wind and rain-proof shell over my winter down jacket. I traded my lightweight hat for my heavier one, and placed a buff (a lightweight scarf) around my neck. I gathered snacks, water bottles, hand warmers, my serious winter mittens. Some things went in my backpack, and other things, for immediate access, into various pockets on my person. I stuck toe warmers onto the tops of my double-stockinged feet before pulling on my hiking boots and then put gaiters over the bottom half of my legs. It took effort to stand upright outside the tent. I grabbed my trekking poles. Craig was quick and ready before I was and had already returned from the toilet tent.

After being served porridge and hot tea, for warmth and sustenance, we trekkers had gathered around Frederick who would be guiding us. It was midnight, the beginning of Sunday, marking our seventh day on the mountain. This was the day my son and I have dreamed about.

Over the years I've had a habit of capturing ideas of places I think I may try to get to and add them to a list on my phone. Two years ago, I'd been browsing this list, Travel Dreams, and saw Kilimanjaro sitting there among several other destinations. I decided to find out more about it, and over the course of many weeks had fun exploring, from the comfort of my home while seated in front of my laptop. It's a popular mountain to climb because anyone who is reasonably healthy can do it. Special mountaineering skills aren't required, and there's no need for ice axes or supplemental oxygen. In the early stages of researching online, I was intrigued by YouTube videos, documentaries, and traveler reviews. Opinions about trekking up Kilimanjaro ranged from it being fairly moderate to extremely challenging. The general recommendation was to be as fit as possible and to be able to tolerate moderately difficult hiking for four to five hours a day. I also found out that you should expect the summit climb to be the hardest thing you'll ever do.

Mainly, what I came away with is that Kilimanjaro is a big mountain. It needs respect, but it is do-able. Oh, and it sounds amazing. I had to decide how badly I wanted to go. What's the tipping point? Do I simply say… yes? I was in excellent health, but getting older by the minute. If I say yes, I should be saying yes and now. For Craig, there was no decision to make—it was always yes. He has an innate travel gene and a strong curiosity for new experiences.

In addition to determining my level of desire to go, I had to look at things like cost, the time factor involved, and whether my fitness level would be up for the task. After extensive pondering, I felt I had a desire to do this trip, but it had to be done sooner rather than later because I was in my late fifties, aging into the status of senior citizen, and it was not something that could wait. Finally, I made a solid decision. I started verbalizing the "K" word, brought it up out of my own thoughts and started sharing it, in late summer of 2018. Verbalizing was the subtle first layer of commitment.

At this time I asked my daughter, Alison, if she'd like to join us. I knew she'd love to see Africa—some magnificent safari and exotic culture would have a strong appeal for her. She adores the beauty of the outdoors tremendously, but in a more comfortable manner. A gorgeous Colorado snowstorm, if she's inside warm and cozy, is just about her favorite kind of weather. And like most people, it is perfectly reasonable to not sign up for an intense physical adventure. I was impressed she gave it some thought before declining. Besides, she already has plenty of adventures under her belt with several family trips over the years.

Hours earlier when we'd set out from Barafu Camp, Frederick instructed me to set out behind him and the first thirty minutes were spent winding through an international collection of tents. I had to be attentive to each step as the ground was loose volcanic rock and scree, in various sizes. It was like walking through the aftermath of thousands of imploded buildings. Not a patch of ground was firm until we got to the packed-down main trail that dissects the campsite in half. Frederick moved at a sloth-like pace, knowing how much energy our group could muster, for which I was grateful, and I wondered at the mental patience it must take for him to go so slowly for us. There is a special saying on Kilimanjaro, *"pole pole"* (pronounced PO lay PO lay), which means slowly slowly. Taking your time getting up the mountain gives you the best chance of reaching the summit.

After trudging through Barafu Camp, we stepped from its perimeter into vast, black darkness. Immediately the mountain turned steep, on an incline that would rival a Colorado black diamond ski run. I tried to steal a glimpse upward but it took energy to do so and felt too easy to lose my balance unless I was concentrating on walking. For the most part I looked down, my headlamp illuminating my steps, and kept resolute to the task at hand.

It feels ridiculous to start out at midnight for the summit, but there are two main reasons why. For most people, it takes six to eight hours to get to the top and getting there at the dawn of day is when the weather is usually clearest which allows for spectacular sunrises and pristine views. The second reason is the itinerary on this summit day is a very long day altogether. After reaching the summit, then returning to Barafu Camp for a brief rest, there are still several hours of down-hiking to reach Mweka Camp, our last camp on the mountain. Summit to Mweka is a nine thousand foot descent, or, another way to put it, we will be hiking from the summit's arctic zone back down to rainforest.

And here we are, our group having followed behind Frederick, more or less in the same order all through the night — myself, Sara, Freddie, then Craig and Ross. We have had three guides trekking with us the whole week, but a fourth one has joined us for this segment in case someone has trouble and needs to turn back.

I don't understand how Frederick stays on the trail. We are surrounded by miles of rocks and boulders, in the dark of night. How can he make out where it is? Sometimes we step up on larger rocks, like climbing up some fairytale giant's staircase. Occasionally, we have to hoist ourselves up onto boulders of various humongous sizes. The zig zag of the trail, the switchbacks, keep going and going and going. Although the experience here is unique, there are many other groups of trekkers all doing the same thing we're doing — trudging along, single-file, *pole pole*. Against deep black of night, the headlamps of those highest up the mountain, the tiniest of lights highest up, seem to blend right into the impossibly starry sky.

During our frequent breaks, I first have to rein in my labored breathing before being able to take a few swigs from my water bottle. The guides have us up and moving again after five minutes so we don't lose body heat. I see Craig only during these intervals, when we are at rest and not moving. I think he's doing okay. I think he's doing better than I am. We have little, inconsequential conversation, just conserving our energy. I don't have any air except for to breathe, so talking is too much effort. The guides keep encouraging us to drink and stay hydrated.

It is dark everywhere so there's not much to see. But when we are resting, I have a chance to stare up into the clear sky. Up here, thousands of feet up into the atmosphere, the sky feels close and its incredible depth is more apparent. The density of the stars boggles my mind. The Milky Way is a bright smear across the sky, over toward the jagged edges of Mawenzi Peak seven miles away. I look at our group. We are collectively exhausted, all operating on very little sleep and all sharing in this great physical effort.

Despair whispers. I am barely aware of the amazement of an imminent summit. Instead, I am having schizoid-like conversations in my head. I begin to think of all the ways this is miserable. I'm exhausted. And cold. Then I scold myself for being a whiner. I try to remind myself why I'm here. Back and forth, I wrestle positive thoughts against despairing ones and I can't tell yet which side is winning.

Our pace is agonizingly slow yet I work for every breath. Like every step is the breathing equivalent of having just run a 50-meter race. We are well into our all-night trek, that period of time between midnight and sunrise. That period of time we humans should be asleep. It is helpful to be a part of a group. The physical aspect is on automatic, and because I'm a part of a group, I cannot entertain doing anything other than continue taking one step at a time. Even though I want to, it's not an option to stop.

This past week, keeping demands of myself to a minimum, I have narrowed down two daily objectives to accomplish— keep walking and stay warm enough. Now, I am thinking, okay I can keep walking. And I do. The warmth part though … this one's harder to hold on to. I have an impressive amount of clothing on, all of which is geared toward keeping warm in cold weather, but my body is tense against the bitter air and the longer into the night, the colder it gets. Well, I think, I'm not meeting the stay-warm-enough objective. So, I just keep walking.

Despair taunts. More time goes by, minutes turn into hours. Everything is up, we only go up, and I'm breathing, gasping, with every step. I place my hiking poles and step, place my hiking poles and step. I do this again and again. All we do is keep slogging along, enduring this prolonged misery. There's nothing to see out here in the darkness, so I cannot distract myself by looking around. I am mentally all-consumed with doing something I just want to quit doing. I cannot think out-side myself. I have no thoughts about Craig or the others in our group or Tanzania or ….

Despair takes over. Sometime along the way, nausea appears. This adds another layer of challenge. I try to think the nausea away, try to talk myself out of it. Maybe if I relax a little, maybe if I breathe a little slower, deeper. If I think about it the right way, it'll be manageable. Throwing up will make it better. Can I make myself throw up? When we stop for a break I wander away and lean over the side of a boulder, willing myself to throw up but am unable to. Yesterday our head guide mentioned the mental aspect of this summit climb is harder than the physical aspect. Yes and no. Mentally, I am having to force myself to continue. But, the physical aspect is pretty darn intense too — walking on a steep mountain slope for hours in arctic cold, laboring for every breath, dealing with nausea … I am using every bit of strength in my body to keep going. I am giving it everything I have to keep moving forward. As we set out again one of the guides starts carrying my backpack for me.

Through my curtain of whining and all-around feeling miserable, I know that physically I'm not to a point where I have to quit. I am not succumbing to severe altitude sickness. But I feel trapped and I want to turn around. It's this lunatic in my head I'm fighting against to push myself to keep going. I force myself to think of reasons to keep going. I don't want to be a quitter, without a good excuse, with my son here. Plus, it would be a downer for the rest of the group too, if I gave up. And, this whole process has been eighteen months in the making, beginning with the idea to do this, through its planning stage, to now, the present moment, with the actual adventure taking place. What a shame if that were wasted. Not to mention a lot of money is involved and a fair amount of work traveling to Tanzania. Family and friends back home are rooting for us and I don't want to disappoint them. Ultimately, these things are the strength, the love, that keep me going.

As we continue, as we get higher, I become so tired I almost feel like I'm sleepwalking. Maybe I am sleepwalking. When I have an occasional coherent thought I think of Craig, only three or four people behind me, but far enough away that we can't communicate. I do not have the energy to turn around to see how he is doing. I hope he's okay. I can barely think beyond my own self.

We are near the top and the guides gather us off the trail again for another break. We find places to sit on large boulders, and I'm surprised to see small plastic mugs being passed around. One of the guides brings out a large thermos.

I look up at Frederick and smile, "Wow!" He pours hot tea into my cup. Hot tea!

Craig holds out his cup with both hands, "Sweet!" and gives a nod of thanks as Frederick fills it.

The sky, below us, hints of dawn with pale horizontal colors appearing behind Mawenzi Peak, the second highest peak on Kilimanjaro. Then we watch as the paleness transforms into vivid colors that are startlingly beautiful, as though a colorful exclamation for a new day. I'm shocked to see the sunrise so soon. Have we already hiked through the night?

I nudge Craig with my elbow, "How ya doin'?" Even at rest we are gasping for air.

"I'm doing good," he says. "We're gonna make it." He sounds strong and sure.

"I was stressing over my nausea," I say. "But now it's gone. Didn't even realize it until now."

"You're gonna make it, Mom."

"I think so," I say.

What a sweet little moment — a short check in with my son, our group gathered around, sipping tea and watching the sunrise.

We get back onto the trail and continue on up. My mind is not present anymore. All I know for sure is that we continued to climb. I do not have memory of our approach up to the crater rim, the topmost portion of the mountain.

Then all of a sudden Frederick looks back at us and says, "We are close, we are almost there." To me this sounds like the gates of heaven opening.

By "there" he means Stella Point. Stella Point is not the summit, but does mark the leveling off of Kilimanjaro where the crater rim of the volcano is a wide flat area, similar to the width of a highway. Yet it is a respectable feat getting this far; for some trekkers this is the farthest they are able to go. How much the assault of high altitude affects your body determines whether you turn back at Stella or keep going. Uhuru Peak is the true summit and is another six hundred feet ahead.

At Stella I feel enormous relief and for the first time am confident I will summit. We are in our last hour of approach to that magic moment of *we made it all the way.* Everything is much better along the crater rim as we walk on hard snowpack, only having to navigate icy ground in a few areas. Up ahead, the curve of the mountain crests and there is just a bit more to go to get to Uhuru. Some people, already having

Me, on left, as we close in on the Summit up ahead. Photo by Craig.

summited and on their way down, call out encouragement as they pass us: You're Almost There! Good Job! You Can Do It!

This Summit Day so far, has been a tremendous challenge. But along the crater rim, this last portion of summiting, is the best part. It is so great! The altitude keeps us at a humble pace, but the incline is gentle. We are not on some scary ridge in danger of falling (not that we have been), but rather on a nice, spacious snowfield. The views, the sky—so spectacular—and it's like you can see forever. Clouds, off behind Mawenzi Peak, are way below us. There are several huge slabs of glaciers off to one side, more long than tall, collectively called the Southern Icefield, and the Reusch Crater, approximately one half mile in diameter, drops down to our right. To our north, we see more snow, more glaciers, and all-around beautiful winter terrain.

Then...

WE ARE HERE! WE MADE IT! We whoop up a little and high-five each other. Everyone is smiling. I give Craig a super big hug. Without him, I wouldn't have even considered this trip and wouldn't be having this amazing experience. And, I am thinking this: I am thankful to have done it, but maybe even more thankful knowing we'll be turning around soon. I am jubilant and exhausted simultaneously.

Since our midnight start, it has taken us eight hours to hike these last three miles to summit.

We have our photos taken at the famous sign:

Mount Kilimanjaro
Congratulations
You Are Now at
Uhuru Peak Tanzania 5895m/19341 ft Amsl
Africa's Highest Point
World's Highest Freestanding Mountain
One of the World's Largest Volcanoes
World Heritage and Wonder of Africa

As soon as we begin our way back, I am practically skipping and am feeling joy, full-on joy.

CHAPTER 2

Puzzles

I n my early twenties I'd moved from my hometown in Michigan to Texas. By my late twenties I'd gotten a Bachelor's degree in OT, began work as an occupational therapist, and met the man of my dreams, James. A big part of our dating life included physical fitness. James and I ran on the seawall in Galveston along the Gulf of Mexico several days a week, and I introduced him to swimming laps at the local Y. After four years, we married.

When we moved to Oklahoma, so James could pursue a new job with an investment company, I was three months pregnant with our firstborn. I cherished the wonder of entering mom-hood and poured lots of energy into making our first home nice (its interior had been in rough condition when we bought it). I kept up with running and swimming, although as my due date drew closer I tapered back with these things. Alison was born and I was as busy as I'd ever been. Caring for our beautiful baby girl was one of the most joyful, but stressful, times for me. Just like everyone with a newborn, those first months were spent in sleep deprivation mode.

Around the time Ali was a year old, I considered getting licensed as an occupational therapist in Oklahoma and return to work. But James was doing well in his career and we didn't have close family nearby so it was an easy decision for me to continue to be a stay at home mom. Craig was born a few years later (arriving three days before Alison's fourth birthday). Yay, now we had a boy too. Because I wasn't overly exhausted with a job outside the home, I was able to really enjoy the role of being a homemaker and caring for our two little ones, plus two cats and a dog. I was on top of the world.

Swimming was a big part of my life because it gave me a strong sense of physical and mental well being. I'd arrive at the Y at 5:30 in the morning and get my workout in before the kids were up for the day. Those thirty minutes in the pool would set me up well for tackling mommy and homemaker duties. Those laps gave me energy to play with the kids too. When they were little, we spent lots of time seeking out parks and playgrounds, and hanging out at the neighborhood pool during the summer. We played a lot.

These little nuggets of activity started small, when the kids were small. Slow and steady, this pattern wove its way into our lifestyle as a family and became more ingrained throughout the years. Eventually leading my son and me to a big mountain in Africa.

Once I decided yes to Kilimanjaro I spent the next year and a half making plans, which was like putting together a thousand-piece jigsaw puzzle, like opening up this huge puzzle and pouring out all the individual pieces onto a table. Starting out, as I made easier, more general decisions, a dim picture began to form of what this trip would look like. I didn't yet know what the end result would be, but I worked on this mountain puzzle, absorbed into spaces within my active life, and watched it begin to take on shape. There would be lots of details to sort out. The Who What When.

The What piece of the puzzle was deciding which of the main six routes to take. I spent a lot of time on this, looking for the one that'd be the best fit for our needs. There are a lot of trekking companies in Kilimanjaro and it took no time at all to become overwhelmed by the plethora of websites catered to getting people to the highest point of Africa. Each site offered tons of information, and each was imbedded with its own bias as being the most successful or safest or fastest. For various reasons, any trail could be the best choice. While still in the early stages of planning I was rescued from some of the deluge of options when I purchased a travel book, *Kilimanjaro: The Trekking Guide to Africa's Highest Mountain,* by a British author named Henry Stedman.

There is a high correlation between the length of the route chosen and a successful summit. Stedman states that a shorter six day route has a 75% summit rate, whereas a nine day route has a 98% summit rate. Going slower allows your heart and lungs to adjust to the ever-decreasing atmospheric pressure as you gain altitude. Considering why we're even planning a trip to Kilimanjaro, getting to the top is, well … a priority. So, I eliminated shorter routes. Obviously, a longer route means more time and expense, but I reasoned summiting on a first attempt would be cheaper than returning for a do-over.

By late 2018 I'd made a few decisions, the When and the What. We would travel in January, 2020, on the Lemosho route which takes eight days. I also wanted to do a brief post-trek safari, something like Arusha National Park, something close and convenient. But I was still figuring out the Who part of the puzzle, who to hire to take us to the top. I was going a little crazy comparing trekking companies —nothing was apple to apple. When I realized I was using one certain guide company to compare all the others with, I made the leap and chose them. By early spring of 2019 I had a solid idea of what this trek would entail and was ready for the next layer of commitment. Putting down a security deposit to the company I selected, our Kilimanjaro idea was closer to becoming a Kilimanjaro reality.

The next several months were filled with tackling trip details and I was keeping as active as possible with swimming, running and hiking. Then all of a sudden, fall was becoming winter and as the weeks raced toward year-end, with our trip scheduled for early 2020, it felt like raking leaves on a windy day keeping track of details. My journal notes captured some of the swirls of anxiety and excitement as the trip approached:

November 21, 2019

Like a teeter-totter I fluctuate between being anxious for things that need to be done and excitement building for the actual adventure. With the passing of time, clearly seen as I update my whiteboard on Fridays (How many days to departure and How many days to Summit), I am prodded to keep up with my to-do list.

Last weekend, Craig helped me process our visas online. Passports, personal photos, and travel itinerary had to be uploaded (way above my computer skills, and Craig too was challenged by this but able to make it happen).

This past Monday, the 18th, I hiked about a 1/4 mile shy of the Flattop Mt summit in Rocky Mountain National Park. Wind was forecast and so I wanted to try out some new gear, a windproof jacket and pants. It was GREAT! I was probably about 11,200 ft and it was crazy windy with occasional powerful gusts. I had to buffer and brace myself against it but the wind wasn't going through my clothes. It felt very comfortable up there. I did manage to lose a glove while I was making a video to show how strong the wind was. Once my glove got away from me, it took off! I watched it for several seconds (it tumbled and flew down the mountain with absolutely nothing to block its path), hoping maybe I could see it land ....

I had an extra pair of gloves in my backpack so my hand didn't freeze on the way back down. Going up and back down was 6.5 miles; took four hours. On this cold, very windy day, I only passed one other hiker until I was back at Bear Lake, at the trailhead.

November 28, 2019

Happy Thanksgiving. Boulder received 22 inches of winter magic two days ago and this morning Craig and I hiked the South Mesa trail in the Boulder foot-hills for three hours. We tested gear. Gaiters (worn on the lower legs to protect against snow, mud, debris); plus Craig has new trekking poles and is still breaking in new hiking boots. I brought my outer shell too, but with zero wind today, it stayed in my backpack.

So lovely! We're both just ready for the wonder of Kili.

Craig and I are facing a little glitch today. Our online visa applications have been approved. However, when we'd filled out the application the Surname box was left blank. Our applications were approved, but they show just our first names! Ugh! Craig sent an inquiry as to how we can edit our visas. (Never got an answer.) Feeling slightly neurotic, I now stress over the thought of not being admitted to their country. A stupid detail that needs to get corrected.

Days to go: 42.

December 7, 2019

I'm just ready to go. This time, when the calendar turned over to December, I didn't have as much anxiety. Rather, resignation. Let's do this.

I've relaxed on the perfectionism that'd crept in. I'm far enough along now to Not Care about a few dangling loose ends.

This week I want to:

    get extra batteries for our headlamps

    determine better our camera situation

    determine how we keep our phones charged on the mountain

I've been working out a lot and feel strong and healthy.

Update on the visa issue. Was relaying my woes to two friends and both said, "I wouldn't worry about it." So... I won't.

December 20, 2019

Have relaxed the Kili planning and have focused on Christmas instead.

January 1, 2020

Happy New Year! Kilimanjaro is days away!

I hiked yesterday, New Year's Eve — 6.5 miles in Rocky Mountain National Park, to Mills Lake and back; temperatures were in the upper 20's.

Hiked another 6 miles this morning, with some wonderful people of the Anthem Ranch Hike Club. Up along Devil's Backbone in Loveland.

January 2, 2020

Anxieties over the trek have subsided greatly. Last summer is when Craig and I started working on the extensive packing list with sleeping gear (sleeping bags, liners, and pads). Then, in October, it was like "work" shopping for necessary clothing. We had to schedule appointments with each other to find time to go to REI for cold-weather clothing. This is no small issue. Warmth on the mountain, especially in extreme weather, equates to being able to enjoy it. Not being warm equates to being miserable.

So, October and November, I had "packing list" anxiety.

Then, in December, I had "tooth" anxiety *(will explain later)*.

Now, one week to go. And only a few details remain, but, oh so manageable. Even Denver's weather forecast looks mild and calm for the 9th.

Anxieties: practically nil.
Excitement: ramping up!

January 4, 2020

We depart in six days.

My tooth feels great.

Did pre-trip laundry yesterday.

Get hair cut tomorrow.

Our guide company is sending frequent emails to guide us through last minute preparations. Things like advising us to pack our hiking boots in our carry-on bags to be sure they arrive with us.

I'm mentally preparing for our travel day Thursday: Ali will pick us up at 3:00 AM to take us to airport.

January 8, 2020

We depart tomorrow in the wee hours of the morning for the airport.

Today the restlessness is practically gone. Stuff actually is fitting into the suitcases. I picture a huge funnel, and gradually, as things are processed, fewer and fewer things remain to be done.

The weather earlier today was sunny, fifty degrees, no wind. I went on a run, 5.5 miles, and it was so wonderful. It was special because I won't be in this familiar territory for a while. Was thinking of how amazingly blessed we are today. Craig nor I are ill or have injury. It is an optimal time for us to go tackle this mountain. With a full day ahead stretched out before me and only minor tasks yet to do, I have the gift of SPACE and CALM. I embrace the wonder of my world so completely changing over the next two weeks. Wow, what a big world.

January 9, 2020

Early morning, on a brisk cold day, Alison drives Craig and me to the Denver airport for our 6:00 AM flight.

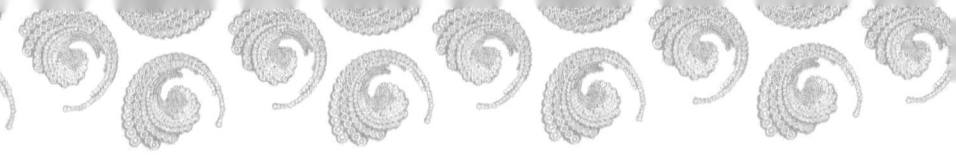

CHAPTER 3

African Soil

We land in Africa on a Friday night. For the most part, it was uneventful traveling from Denver to New York to Amsterdam to Tanzania. We passengers file off the KLM Royal Dutch aircraft, down steep stairs, from both front and rear exits, and onto the tarmac. Some disembarking tourists interrupt the flow of people to stop and take pictures of the big blue bird, which seems almost as large as the airport itself. Craig and I get funneled through the automatic sliding doors of Kilimanjaro International Airport which was built in 1971 to accommodate tourists coming in to see majestic wildlife or climb a certain big mountain.

After only minor confusion getting through customs and retrieving our checked luggage, we step out into the humid warmth of African night. A small crowd is gathered outside waiting to greet arrivals. Almost immediately we see a stocky, older gentleman holding a small sign with a cartoonish picture of a rhinoceros wearing a red hiking boot. The sign has our names in big print under the logo, so Craig and I walk up and introduce ourselves to him.

"*Karibou!* Welcome! I'm Willie," he says, with a gentle smile. "I'm your driver."

"Nice to meet you," we say. Shaking hands with Willie, we cross the threshold into the care of our guide company.

He leads us a short distance to an avocado green Land Rover that looks as though it's got a few safaris under its belt. We are headed to an area known as Mbahe, about two hours away, which is tucked in the foothills of Africa's famous mountain. The owner of the guide company I hired has converted part of his family's farm into the Mbahe Cottages, a kind of bed and breakfast set-up, for travelers in his care. We will have a few easy days of leisure before the start of our climb.

We get settled into the Rover. Willie puts our luggage in the far back and makes sure we are comfortable and ready to go. Exiting the airport, he describes how we'll be going through Moshi Town before arriving in Mbahe. His English is good but layered in heavy accent, so I strain to listen carefully. We are the foreigners in his country, so I suppose it's Craig and me with the heavy accents. It's not far to Moshi and most noticeable to me, as we're driving through it, is how dark it is. Absent are street lights or much public lighting of any kind. I'm used to electricity just being there. Here, it's used selectively and has a limit. Although it's not well lit and it's hard to see, this town of about a hundred fifty-thousand is full up with activity.

Willie is a smooth driver, with apparent owl-like vision, and glides easily through the bustling movement of cars, bikes, motorbikes and scooters. A lot of people are walking on the dirt shoulders of the road, only steps from the pavement of the street, and it makes me nervous because they're so close to traffic and they're hard to see. It's a kind of ordered disorder.

In some areas I can make out people gathered outside in small groups sitting in chairs around tables, hanging out. What lights I do see in homes or buildings, it seems only a room or two are lit, using low wattage. A couple of times we pass a big scene with loud music and many bright lights, night clubs in action on this Friday night, where there's serious partying.

I want to be polite and make conversation, but with street noises, the vehicle's engine and my fatigue, it's difficult to understand what Willie is saying and after a while my chit chat tapers off. The minutes feel long. I glance over at Craig, dozing, snuggled up against his side door. It's like he has some innate travel gene that allows him to be carefree in the face of new experiences into the unknown. He seems to ride out the discomforts of traveling with ease. We are so weary from long flights and he simply retreats into sleep next to me. Not a feather ruffled.

I watch the scenery through my window and after a while urban activity fades into rural stillness. City streets narrow into two-lane roads, and at one point, on a steep, curved hill we spend several minutes following behind a large truck, in first and second gears. Willie is effortlessly patient and I am too. What's the hurry?

James changed jobs in 2000 and our family moved to Northern Kentucky, just outside Cincinnati, when the kids were eight and four. Taking advantage of living in that area, we visited a lot of U.S. historical sites, which were a big interest to James. I also sought out the pretty places and checked out different parks and trails with the kids. Once in a while we'd take a whole day to explore state parks and get on a trail some-where beautiful. Several times, we visited Mammoth Cave

National Park. Wild, beautiful places settle my mind and bring awe to my senses.

I hungered to see things and appreciated moving to wherever James' work took him so we could spend significant time learning about a new area. The kids learned to snow ski in southern Indiana, a half hour's drive from our house, at Perfect North Slopes. Relative to an actual mountain, these were big hills, with an elevation of eight hundred feet, but we had a blast skiing almost every week in winter. Our first adventure travel, the kids twelve and eight at the time, was a long weekend on a guided white water rafting trip in West Virginia. It was crazy exciting.

The very last bit to the cottages is a narrow dirt track, deeply rutted from recent rains. Craig becomes alert for this as we slow to a crawl and bounce over large potholes. Willie has to scout out certain areas, stopping the Rover and ever so slowly climbing up and over muddy ruts. Craig and I both hold tight to the grab handles above our car doors. My legs are freely swinging back and forth as we go over the bumps and at one point my knee connects with the edge of a metal storage box on the floor between our seats. EEE OUCH!

The road ends at a small river and we park in front of a pedestrian bridge where a few staff are waiting for us to help with our luggage. Craig and I are ready with headlamps for a quick ten minute walk up a narrow path to the Mbahe cottages.

"Craig!" I say, turning slightly so he can hear me. "We've been preparing for this for so long and now we're here."

"This place looks really cool," he says. "It's like an outpost in the jungle. Like something you'd see in Jurassic Park."

"You're right, that's a good way to put it." I give Craig a quick hug, "I'm happy I get to do all this with you."

I imagine Ali back in Colorado. She would enjoy being immersed in a place so very different from what we're used to. However, she isn't ever far away from a good book and I'm sure she's taking advantage of the solitude of us being away. Also, the whisper of the idea of returning to school for her Master's is taking hold and I know she's giving that some serious thought.

It's around 11:00 PM when Abraham, our host, greets us at the main gate of the Mbahe Cottages. He is tall (and may I add, dark and handsome), well-dressed and articulate. We are offered simple refreshments and asked to be seated at a heavy wooden table, one of the few large tables in an outdoor lounge and dining area.

Abraham briefs us on procedures they use to monitor our health. He applies an oximeter to my index finger, then Craig's, and records our oxygen levels on separate charts on a clipboard. They will monitor how well our bodies adjust as we go up in altitude over the course of the next several days. Abraham also makes note that we are taking Diamox, a high altitude prophylactic, and they will track our daily use of it.

He reiterates what I've read many times already, that it's crucial to keep hydrated. To keep as physically healthy as possible means we'll be expected to drink at least three liters of water every day. Craig and I each have a couple of 32 ounce Nalgene water bottles so we're to drink the equivalent of three of those. Our fluid intake will be recorded on our charts also. Our guide company refers to these particulars as "smart altitude management."

The most important factor in summiting is being able to deal with ever-increasing altitude. Basically, the best things to do are drink well, eat well, rest well. And to take it slow. However, even if you do all the right things, something as innocent as a change in medicine, say, blood pressure medicine, may end up preventing someone from being able to complete the whole trek.

Abraham shows us our room. Generated electricity is set to expire so we brush our teeth and collapse into our beds before running out of light. Candles and matches are provided but I'm in a hurry anyway to get to bed. My body craves being stretched out flat and my mind craves to be turned to OFF mode. After thirty-six hours of hurtling across three continents, I melt into the promise of luxurious sleep.

I wake up Saturday morning feeling refreshed. Our room is simple, in a rustic, elegant kind of way, furnished with two full-sized beds and a nightstand in between. Of course, the highest bar, the true indicator of how nice accommodations are, is determined by what the shower is like. The bathroom takes up one length of our square room, a curtain for the door, with the commode at one end, the sink in the middle portion, and the shower capping off the other end. A small lip along the floor and a shower curtain defines this space. I turn on the faucet and step under warm, heavy water pouring out from a shower head, the size of a dinner plate, hanging straight down from the ceiling… a virtual spa experience.

Craig and I are the only guests. The cottages are made up of three one-story buildings comprising eight rooms altogether. When we're all showered and dressed, we take a look through a door at the back of our room, stepping onto a porch shared with two other rooms of our building, which is built into a steep hillside. Thick forest is within arms reach and we can hear a rushing river below, but it's mostly hidden by a wall of foliage.

Over a year ago, when the idea of Kilimanjaro was taking shape, as I researched, I got onto some rabbit trails; there were so many possibilities for designing this trip. Traveling all the way to Africa—you just have to take advantage of the fabulous wild life. Places like the Serengeti, Angorogora Crater, and Endutu. I became consumed with how to work in a safari for us. I processed options by writing down thoughts in my journal:

> Do we climb Kilimanjaro and finish with a safari, combining two big trips into one enormous one?
>
> Do we have Ali fly here and join us for the safari part?
>
> Or do I just do Kilimanjaro with my son?
>
> Do I wait and come back to Africa with her and do a safari?
>
> I decided I didn't like the idea of two significant trips combined into one. It would be too complicated, costly, and time consuming.
>
> I decided to just focus on planning a mountain climb.
>
> I cannot commit to it, but I hope I get back to Africa with my daughter someday for a big beautiful safari.

We head over for breakfast at our appointed time. The walkways of the cottages are lined with narrow ditches and in some areas pipes go underneath the walks to direct the flow of water, making allowances for this area's rainy seasons. It takes us less than a minute to walk through the center of the cottages, through the middle of vegetable and flower gardens that take up every inch of space available. From a daylight perspective now, the dining area has generous views. Beyond the tall fence enclosing the cottages, portions of heavy forest meet up with cultivated farm land. In one direction, beyond the immediate area of the farm, we have forever views down and away from here.

Last night we had ordered our breakfast from a small paper menu, choosing from a variety of omelets and a few a la carte items, such as pastries and fruit. One of the omelet choices allows you to pick your own herbs from the garden that we had just walked through, which I thought was really cool. We meet our server, a quiet gentleman named Romanos. He's of average height but has a characteristic stoop of an older person you sometimes see. He has already set up two place settings on the table and an impressive coffee bar on a large counter off to the side. I fill my cup with Mbahe-grown coffee, adding cocoa powder and steamed milk. At the far end of the counter, is a large stainless steel dispenser with filtered water for whenever we need to fill our Nalgene bottles. Like the habit of never going anywhere without a cell phone, here, we'll never go anywhere without our water bottles.

Abraham appears and calls out, "Good morning! *Jambo!*" Hello! He makes a big presence with his height and suave looks. He seems to be in his late thirties, early forties.

"*Jambo!*" Craig and I say, giggling a little with our Swahili.

"Before you eat, I need to get your oxygen levels," he says and we take turns with the oximeter. "Also," Abraham says, "I introduce to you a breathing game. You are to count your breaths, while I time you, for one minute. One breath in and one breath out equals one respiration."

It feels impossible to breathe naturally while deliberately counting, but we do our best. He asks how much we have had to drink since last night. He asks have we taken our Diamox today. He records all this on our charts.

Romanos brings out hearty banana bread and a platter of sliced fruit—oranges, mangoes, bananas—wonderfully sweet, perfectly ripe. The kitchen is close by in a separate building and he paces back and forth between it and the dining area, laden with food which is fresh from the hills of this small village.

This food is like affirmation that we are with a good guide company. Having to choose among so many companies and so many variables, with things like length of trail, itineraries, and optional add-ons, was tough. I came up with three priorities to look for—utmost attention to our safety, the best possibility for a summit, and good working conditions for the crew. Because climbing a mountain has inherent physical risk, safety was my top priority (it would not be good if Craig or I were to die). Next, our objective for going to Kilimanjaro was getting to the top and I wanted us to have the best shot possible to achieve that. My third biggest concern, regarding the crew, stemmed from learning about the Kilimanjaro Porters Assistance Project (KPAP) which supports ethical treatment of those working on the mountain.

I ended up following the line of a domino put before me. My friend, Roger, had summited Kilimanjaro several years ago with his daughter. He referred me to a safari company who in turn referred me to Simon Mtuy, a gentleman they get in touch with if their clients have interest in Kilimanjaro. Simon grew up at the base of the mountain and worked as a guide before starting his own climbing company in 1998, called Summit

Expeditions and Nomadic Experience, or SENE (pronounced SEN ay). Having started with this loose personal connection to SENE, sitting in the dining area this morning and enjoying fresh, homegrown food, I'm quite happy—we are eating well, in this glorious place, in the hands of an outstanding company.

"Looks like we won't be eating processed food for a while," Craig says.

There has already been plenty of food but when Romanos shows up with our omelets, I remember we have only gotten started. Setting our omelets in front of us, with bacon on the side, he says, "Would you like more banana bread? More fruit?" He's on alert for anything we may want more of.

"No, this is wonderful, this is perfect," Craig says while motoring through everything in front of him.

Since we arrived in Africa last night we have been treated so well. I'm about to ask where my robe and tiara are ....

I have two Rotary Club flags from Boulder, Colorado, given to me by Roger, my domino connection. As we finish breakfast, I ask Abraham if he can pass these flags along to Simon, who, in addition to several hats he wears, is also president of the local Marangu rotary club. It's a thing, Rotary Clubs exchanging flags all over the world.

You can't describe Simon Mtuy as ordinary. He's a rotary club guy and also runs this guide company which, in addition to summit treks up Kilimanjaro, offers safaris and foothill treks. He also hosts an annual Kilimanjaro Stage Run for elite athletes. An elite athlete himself, he travels extensively as an ultra marathoner and participates in hundred mile races. And, he's raising a family. I've never had a groupie adoration of anyone before, but must admit I am a bit in awe. Now that we're here I've been hoping to get a glimpse of him, but don't want to push myself on him.

I really don't want breakfast to end, but next on our agenda is for Abraham to show us around the Mbahe farm village, and we make plans to meet up with him in a short while. It's quiet around the cottages and we see a few people working on the property. There's a woman sweeping the dirt paths with a primitive short-handled broom, bent over at the waist. Someone else is tending the herb garden. And another man, with a large pair of shears, is trimming a square of lawn by the entrance gate.

Coming back from a brief time in our room we see Abraham waiting for us near the cottage gate.

"Ready to see the farm?" he asks, with a wide, generous smile.

"We're ready!"

He opens the gate for us. There are a couple of grazing cows nearby and we walk past them on a foot-worn path down toward the main Mbahe community, the same path we'd come up last night. It's a partly cloudy day and feels like sixty degrees or so. It feels great to be moving again after having been confined in the seats of airplanes for so long.

We come to the pedestrian bridge and see it is built several feet high over a river, a hint of how major the weather must be like during rainy season. A memorial plaque reads, "The Bridge of Life." Abundant growth is everywhere, farm land competing for space with rainforest. Abraham shares with us that this farm flourishes because of the climate and abundance of water. "And," he says, "the ways of doing things, like crop rotation and paying attention to how one type of crop

can benefit another, has been carried on for generations."
He walks us through banana, coffee, sweet potato, corn and
pumpkin crops.

We are no longer near the river but I hear the sound of
water, and Craig and I notice narrow ditches on either side
of the path we're on, water running down from the slopes of
Kilimanjaro and directed for crops. Abraham tells us these
ditches are part an irrigation system, perfected over time and
used for over a hundred years.

"Wow," I say, "I feel miniature inside a world of Paul Bunyan."

"Look at the corn—it's more than twice as tall as we are."
Craig says.

Abraham smiles, "Amazing, isn't it?" He gestures uphill,
"I'll take you back now. Did you enjoy the tour?"

"Yes, thanks for showing us around," I say. "It's so beautiful."

How lovely, the Mbahe-style demands we are burdened
with—breakfast, a nice walk, and now it's time for lunch.
In the dining area, Craig and I relax. We notice dark clouds
marching in, so I hurry to our room to fetch rain jackets and
return just in time to appreciate a fierce downpour from under
the protection of the over-sized roof above us. Romanos serves
lunch, doing his best to bring our food from the kitchen,
huddling under the eaves to avoid getting soaked. The rain
is heavy, but brief, and doesn't interfere with our afternoon
agenda which is for Abraham to show us more of the village.

A short time later, bellies content, we set out again. Modest
homes are tucked into hills and crevices, most of them hidden
under massive flora, as though the village is swallowed into the
folds of farm and forest. What an absolute treat to see the way
of life in this part of the world. Before too long, a small boy

A modest home in Mbahe village. Photo by Ross.

runs toward us, coming up the narrow path from his home, waving his hand, "*Jambo!*"

Laughing, Craig and I respond, "*Jambo!*"

I feel conspicuous and on display, we pale foreigners walking through this farm community, as other women and small children come out to watch us pass by. Especially the small children are excited to see us, waving and smiling. There are Hellos and Welcomes all around: "*Jambo!*" or "*Karibou!*" After a fairly short while we return to the cottages. The calm of Mbahe village beckons us to leave behind our western fast-paced culture and to embrace, what feels to me, a more reasonable pace of life. I can easily get behind the Tanzanian proverb, "Hurry, hurry has no blessings."

Another American family arrives in late afternoon, looking a bit travel-worn. Abraham, in his gracious way, sets about welcoming them, and straight off gets their oximeter readings.

We meet Ross, perhaps about thirty-five years old, and his niece and nephew, Sara and Freddie. I like that they are close in age to Craig, in their early twenties. This is who we will trek with to the top of Kilimanjaro. At sixty, I'm older than Ross by at least twenty-five years and older than the "kids" by at least thirty-five. Someone has to be the oldest, right? I don't feel out of my league with this group because I've had good health my whole life and I've developed stamina while hiking in the Rocky Mountains since moving to Colorado six years ago.

There's a quiet lull for a few hours before we five are gathered together for dinner. The three newbies are rather quiet and reserved, a lot like Craig and me. We have small talk. How was your flight, where you guys from, et cetera. Weeks ago, I'd read someone's account of their Kilimanjaro experience. Their whole group had summited and the trek went okay, but the toxic dynamics of the other family they were with affected everyone's ability to *hakuna matata*. Not that I expect that, but I sure hope these people we're with are nice.

Magic is being cooked up from the kitchen building and Romanos keeps bringing us large amounts of delicious food. The main course is a light, delicate fish. I'm overwhelmed with how good everything is. Afterwards, Craig and I retreat to an alcove at the far end of the dining area, where there's a large fireplace flanked by a couple of cozy reading chairs. Large canvas flaps can be brought down to enclose the space if it's cold, but tonight's weather is comfortable. There's a tall book-shelf with a handful of games and books, including an edition of Henry Stedman's guidebook and a photo book put together by someone who'd stayed here.

We go back to our room and putter about separating mountain gear and clothing from all the other things we'd brought. Our suitcases hold everything we need to get us through these two days on the farm, eight days on the mountain, one full day on safari, and finally, three days worth of travel back to the States. We had packed a lot of hiking gear, and clothing for every type of weather, from tropical to arctic. We'd already had what felt like arctic conditions on our last travel leg, on KLM Royal Dutch Airlines — even grown men shivered like babies it was so cold on the flight down here.

It's well after dark. Dinner is finished and we've organized our gear a little, so the only thing left to do is go to bed.

"Good night, Craig. Love you."

"Good night, Mom. Love you too."

CHAPTER 4

Coffee

Good morning, Sunday. I wake up without relief of a decent night's sleep, but of course morning coffee comes to the rescue. Tanzanians have a word for its wake-up properties, which translates into "slap." Craig and I head for the dining area and boy, do I relish that first cup. We are joined there by the rest of our group. Ross looks very fit and my impression is Adventure must be in his DNA. It was his idea to ask Sara and Freddie to tag along with him to climb Kilimanjaro.

Sara is a tall redhead and immediately I appreciate her animated personality. In the short amount of time since I've met her, she seems like someone easy to get along with. She had just completed a nursing degree last month and I wonder how she managed to get ready for this trip and take finals all at the same time. Her brother, Freddie, more of a listener and observer, has an understated manner and I think is still tired from all the travel. At times though, his quick, dry wit seeps through.

Before Romanos serves breakfast, Abraham goes through the ritual of recording blood oxygen levels and respirations, and it gives me a lot of comfort having our health monitored and knowing we'll be watched carefully during our climb.

"Remember to drink plenty of water today," Abraham says, "and keep track of how much." He asks Craig and me if we'd taken our Diamox. Of the five of us, we are the only ones using it.

Diamox is on SENE's extensive packing list, and described as "effective against the symptoms of altitude sickness." When I looked into it, I couldn't find anything about the drug that was unequivocally yay or nay on its effectiveness. Because it's hard to measure how someone is affected by high altitude in the first place, it's hard to measure how well the drug works. As a prophylactic, it affects the bloodstream in a way that stimulates more rapid breathing which supposedly causes more oxygen to get to your bloodstream. For Craig and me, I decided we should take it, but who's to know if this will give us an edge during our climb.

"Yeah, we took it this morning," I say. "I have a bit of tingling in my fingers. A little buzzy feeling around my mouth from it." This is a minor side effect some people get.

"That's not happening to me," Craig says. A minute later, "Dang it, Mom, now my fingers are tingling!"

As Abraham wraps up with each of our health sheets, the food shows up. Romanos brings platters of sliced fruit for us. Fresh, sweet, delicious.

Sara says, "Awesome!"

He brings out banana bread and bacon. Sara, "Awesome!"

He brings out our omelets. "Awesome!"

I like Sara. She makes me laugh.

While we eat, Abraham tells us a little about himself. He grew up in Tanzania, has a young family, was educated in London, something like a business degree, and enjoys being host at Mbahe. "But someday," he says, "I hope to guide groups up the mountain." While he shares with us, he's also paying attention to how much we eat, monitoring our appetites. Food intake is another part of altitude management noted on our charts.

After breakfast we go over to a nearby building which houses the kitchen and are invited to step inside. There's no room to spare with all of us standing around and it's like we're in someone's personal home kitchen.

"Please," Abraham says, "Meet Leonardo, our cook."

Leonardo is thin and half the size as Abraham. He's wearing a white apron and tall chef's hat, both, a bright contrast against his dark chocolate skin. I whisper to Craig that he's the most important member of the crew.

Leonardo also wears an enormous smile. "*Karibou!* Welcome! How do you like the food?" The wealth of food he prepares is sourced at this Mbahe farm—coffee, bread, eggs, fruits and vegetables. A few things, like meat and fish, he gets from the local market.

We stand there, smiling, and tell him how wonderful the food is, "*Asante!*" Thank you!

Our morning's plan is another walk through Mbahe. We leave the kitchen, scatter back to our rooms for a short time, and meet back up at the communal balcony centered in the middle of the cottages. This covered balcony is like an outdoor family room. It has built-in seating along its perimeter with thick comfy seat cushions and pillows, and a large, low table in the middle. It juts out from the hillside, supported by large support beams on its far end, several feet high. On one side, we have spectacular views of the farm sloped downward from the cottages and of sky that reaches out for miles. On the other side, we are enclosed by the rustic cottages in the middle of the herb and vegetable gardens.

A snapshot of several decades of my life would show me raising two children and managing our home, and being active with fitness, playing and exploring. My time was my own, a blank slate of sorts, and within the limitations of our family's activities, I could spend time however I wanted. I didn't want it to go to waste sitting home watching soap operas, so I also did a lot of volunteer work. In part, volunteering was a form of active gratitude I had for the privilege of so much freedom.

Those days were layered with helping out at the kids' schools and countless opportunities to serve at church. When our young family lived in Oklahoma I volunteered at the local donation center for families needing a handout with food and clothing (Ali was a toddler then and she'd help out too). Later, in Texas, I was a volunteer in the epidemiology department at the huge Baylor University Medical Center in Dallas. Over the course of several years and across several states where we've lived (Texas, Oklahoma, Kentucky and again, Texas), I've donated gallons of blood platelets. In Texas and overlapping into Colorado, I'd spent ten years advocating for victims of child sex trafficking.

I grew to love going on trips. Traveling gave me a break from routine and provided an escape from daily responsibilities. Our family seemed to have an unending line of trips in the queue and I had fun planning all of them. I would be happy just to know we had someplace to go, to have that special something to look forward to.

Just beyond the cottages, two black cows are grazing.
Nearby is a lone acacia tree, standing proud and elegant, and I
ask Craig to take a picture of it for me. Waiting for Abraham,
in this serene setting, I'm enjoying each moment. I'm pretty
good at the art of relaxing, and the slow walks and good food
we've been treated to offers us a nice rebound from the tension
of the days leading up to this trip. It feels like I've been rehears-
ing for a play for months, the hard work of it, and now the
performance is being played out. The simple act of Craig taking
a picture of the acacia tree is like a letting go of the cares of the
world.

In the days leading up to our flight I was restless, in constant motion attending to this detail, or that. Had my hair cut
to a no-fuss mountain doo (read: very short), purchased more
AA batteries for our camera and more socks for Craig. I was
intent on making sure our feet were happy, so having several
pairs of decent quality socks helps deter sores and blisters.
I made sure to remind Craig to trim his toenails too. I kept
finding little things to check off my list. Made sure all my bills
were scheduled to be paid. The day before our flight was when
I actually started packing. For months, as we checked items
off SENE's packing list, the empty middle bedroom at home
was the staging area for our on-going accumulation of stuff,
the floor disappearing under it all. So packing simply meant
putting into suitcases everything that'd been piled up there.

The lone acacia tree—reflects my calm heart.

We begin a leisurely walk, again on footpaths that weave
through an abundance of crops. Abraham describes what
we're seeing. Bananas, beans, beehives. The beehives are short,
hollowed out logs and he points out a few that are perched

impossibly high in treetops. There is lots and lots of corn. We go down a steep hill to the beautiful Moonjo river. It's so steep, and the grass slick with moisture, that I wish I had trekking poles. At the base of the hill a grand waterfall empties into an area, roughly the size of your local pool at the YMCA, and greets us with light spray before continuing its meander. Sometimes swimming is permitted, but with significant rainfall the past few days, the torrent is too dangerous. Brrrr! I am not feeling bad about it. We sit on big rocks on a large curve of the river smack in the middle of tranquility. We gaze up at the roaring falls. I gaze up into the sky, mesmerized by clouds, the big fluffy I-see-a-dragon kind. The water roars too loud for conversation. I like the other family we're with and it looks like they are just trying to take it all in too, and probably still recovering from their long flights.

In 2006, our family moved to Texas, to the Fort Worth area, not too far from where James grew up. Here, Alison entered high school, and Craig, fifth grade. After our white water experience in West Virginia a few years before, James and I set our sights on rafting the Grand Canyon, but we had to wait until Craig was twelve to do the gnarliest part of it. In the summer of 2008, with OARS rafting company, we put in at Lee's Ferry and did the first one hundred miles of the canyon to Phantom Ranch. The thrill level on the river was ten out of ten. I craved more.

Craig and I arrived at the cottages a whole day before the other three. When I'd booked our flights last March, in 2019, we were in the midst of a blizzard in Colorado, dubbed the "Bomb Cyclone," which resulted in hundreds of canceled flights at Denver International Airport. Absolutely I wanted to factor in an extra day of travel for this trip to reduce the possibility of missing out on the trek. Turns out, the weather last Thursday was ideal getting out of Denver, and we had zero issues the whole way. Darn, we get to spend another day in paradise for no reason. If Alison were here, she'd love this place. She'd love the slow motion of time. I wonder what she'd see in the fluffy clouds above.

We'd decided on the month of January to climb. Kilimanjaro has two dry seasons, January to mid-March and June to October. It was easy to rule out the sloppier wet seasons because hiking in rain isn't pleasant and heavy dense clouds limit views. Their January to mid-March dry season is summertime in the southern hemisphere, making it a slightly warmer time to go, although being so near the equator, the temperature doesn't fluctuate much. However, because this trek takes you into arctic-type conditions at 19,341 feet, I opted for as much warmth as possible. January also worked well for Craig's school schedule, and so that's how the When piece of the puzzle was nudged into place.

Roused from the waterfall rest stop, we continue exploring up and down the rolling layout of the farm, mostly on narrow little paths, sometimes on a dirt road. Cows are tethered on long ropes, getting moved about by their herders periodically for access to water or another pasture. At times, we see villagers tending the lush crops, mainly by hand, or women washing clothes in a stream. Although some things seem more primitive than what I'm used to seeing, cellphones are everywhere. I see a man far out in a field tending crops and looking down at a cell phone in exactly the same way me or my kids would look down at our phones while in the middle of doing something else.

Going down a short steep hill I slip and fall backwards, but catch myself before landing in the mud on my butt. Agh! I'm not even on the mountain yet. Abraham is quick to ask if I'm alright and then says it's time to bring us back to the cottages. We have some free time and the five of us travelers end up at the communal balcony, arranged languidly along the seating around its edges. I jot down thoughts in my notebook, up against a corner with my legs stretched full-out. Craig reads, laid out at the other end of the bench. Ross and Sara, hunched over the low table, invite us to play Scrabble, but we decline. Freddie naps. There is minimal conversation and time goes by slowly, splendidly. The two black cows are again near the acacia tree. Clouds begin to gather and darken, headed our way.

Scribbling notes, on the balcony, I am so relaxed. While putting this trip together I was—happily—stressed with working our Kilimanjaro Puzzle. Researching the area allowed me to learn more about the mountain and Tanzania, things like geology, wildlife and culture. The more I looked into Africa, the more I fell in love with it. How's the best way to see this faraway, beautiful country? Sitting here now, I get to just let everything play out. We have two full days of rest here at Mbahe before setting out on the eight day Lemosho route.

Lunch is announced and we trade the balcony for the dining area. Leonardo and Romanos provide a five-star feast, and afterward we are treated to the Chagga technique of how coffee is made, from ground to cup. We stand outside near the kitchen while Abraham and Romanos explain how beans are picked and shelled by hand. Nearby, on a large piece of canvas, the size of a living room rug, beans are set out to dry in the yard. Earlier, I saw someone quickly fold it up and remove it when rain came in. Using a few handfuls of shelled beans Abraham places them in a deep wooden mortar on the ground and we watch as Romanos sits down and holds it tight between his feet. He then grind the beans with a pestle the size of a baseball bat. Stepping into the kitchen, they allow me to put the grounds in an ordinary household coffee maker, add water and push the button. I get all the credit for making great coffee. Coffee beans grown here are only sold to guests at Mbahe and I put in an order for a few bags to take home with me. Slightly more caffeinated now, we place our empty cups in the sink.

Abraham asks, "Are you ready for another tour through the village?"

"Yes, yes, of course," we say.

Going in a different direction this time, we see lots of children out and about, older ones making their way home from school, or church, I'm not sure. Some stand and watch as we

Craig, me, Sara, Freddie and Abraham. Photo by Ross.

walk by, maybe giving a shy wave. Others wave with enthusiasm and call out *Jambo!* We see a partially constructed church on a hillside overlooking the valley stretching below. As the body of parishioners grows, another piece of building is added and, according to Abraham, it's been at least ten years in the making. I don't see signs of any large construction equipment. Or signs of any particular rush to complete the project. It's just being steadily built, as needed.

Further along, a girl about the age of ten, approaches me, "Welcome, hello," she says and politely shakes my hand. With the style of an ambassador, she greets the others as well, one by one shaking hands with everyone. I am struck how self-assured she is. It also feels as if she's conveying an appreciation from the community itself, as though our presence as tourists is welcome, and that we have a favorable impact on their quality of life. I hope that's true.

A narrow path takes us past a simple, three-stall pen occupied by a cow, its calf, and an enormous pig. Abraham stops to talk to a man who is scrubbing the pig with a big brush and lots of sudsy water, as though washing a prized car. He looks to be having the time of his life, smiling big, as he and Abraham converse for a few minutes in their tribal tongue. A teenaged girl is helping the man, fetching a pail of water from the stream steps away from the pens. They are in no hurry and all the while they talk, the man keeps scrubbing the pig. I think the pig is smiling too, subject to a vigorous massage. I don't ask if the bacon we had this morning has a name.

Back near the cottages again, Abraham brings us through more of Simon's homestead and we see several homes of his extended family. Although these separate family compounds are essentially connected to each other, tall fencing and heavy forest provide privacy. Nearby is a small, well-groomed cemetery.

About a hundred yards before returning to the front gate of Mbahe, we pass a group of young adults sitting on the hillside looking out over a beautiful vista, as though they are relaxing after a hard day's work. They are passing around fermented maize, all sharing from one large jar, much the way a group of friends would pass around a joint. They invite us to try some. I take a sip from the jar. It tastes like alcohol but with bits in it, like pulp. It isn't all that good, but it's nice being welcomed into a little bit of their world and being offered something personal.

"*Asante*," I say and place a hand over my heart.

At the cottage gate, Abraham bids adieu and the lull in activity draws us five to the main balcony again. Whether active and exploring the farm, or quiet and resting, I'm thrilled to be in Africa, appreciating every moment. Fairly soon Abraham approaches us; a young man is with him and our small group becomes alert.

"Everyone, this is Tim," Abraham says. The gentleman by his side is slender, with youthful good looks, and I'm guessing he's in his early thirties. "He'll be your head guide on the mountain."

"*Jambo*," he greets us, shaking hands with each of us in a rather formal, business-like manner. Right away he asks, "Would you like me to show you our route?"

We nod eagerly. He unfolds a large trail map of Kilimanjaro and flattens it out on the low table. We five circle around, enthralled, as he traces the Lemosho route, right on up to the lazy curlycue of the summit, and explains how our next several days will play out. Tim describes how the route approaches the mountain from the west, travels through rainforest, and comes to the Shira Plateau which takes two days to cross. The trek continues to Lava Tower and the Barranco Wall (SENE's website calls the Wall "a challenging and exhilarating rock scramble"). After the Wall, the route connects through the Karanga valley, goes up to Barafu, and ends at Uhuru Peak, the highest point in all of Africa. Uhuru means "freedom" in Swahili.

We oh and ah a little and ask a few questions. Seeing our route and talking to Tim makes my heart beat faster, the Big Trek imminent. Straightening up, Tim says he wants to see all the gear we plan to have with us on the mountain. He looks at his watch and gives us a few minutes to go to our rooms to prepare for show and tell, and we all head off to go do that. Minutes later there's a tap tap on our door frame and Tim and Abraham step inside. After they give a visual sweep of our stuff laid out on our beds, Craig and I then pack it all into our duffles so they can be weighed with a luggage scale. Crews working on the mountain are limited to carrying a certain amount of weight in total.

When everyone has passed the gear test, we meet up for dinner. We eat inside tonight, in a small dining room adjacent to the kitchen, because torrential rain is pouring out of the clouds. A low-grade current of excitement and nervousness hovers.

Abraham says, "You're on your way tomorrow. You'll do great!"

We're a quiet group and it's hard to get a read on what others are thinking. Ready and confident? Or nervous? Or terrified? I'm ready, but nervous.

Someone asks, "Can you run us through what our day looks like for tomorrow?"

"Be prepared to leave here at 6:15 in the morning," Abraham says. "Have all your things packed. There'll be porters to carry your luggage down to the Land Rover. Willie will be there to drive you."

Abraham explains that our valuables —cash, passports, drivers licenses—will be kept at the SENE office, in Moshi. I know to expect this. We'd been told, in travel correspondence, our valuables are to be held in a secure place. Still, a bit of, no … *lots of* trust is required here. To trust that it's safer not to have our valuables with us on the mountain. We have a few more questions and Abraham calmly answers each one. I feel our group has a good grasp of what's ahead.

Wrapping up, he says, "So, after stopping at the offices to store what you don't need on the mountain, Willie will take you to the Londorossi Gate." He's referring to one of the western entrances of Kilimanjaro.

Our meal is finished and we start to leave to go back to our rooms for the night. "See you back here at 5:15 for breakfast," Abraham says.

"Goodnight everyone!" we call out to each other.

Tomorrow will be a busy day, with final details getting checked off the list before we take our first single step on the mountain.

It's. Getting. So. Close.

CHAPTER 5

First Steps

Monday, day one on the mountain.

The alarm sounds at 4:15 AM. It had rained most of the night, long and steady. Although I'd felt cozy and safe, I didn't sleep well. During the night, the sound of rain was steps away on the other side of the thin wall of our room. I remember hearing distant thunder, and then rain came on by bucketloads, dropping out of the sky heavy, as though the Moonjo River was pouring out over the corrugated roof. Oh boy, I thought, this is the day we'll be setting off for eight days of trekking, eating and camping in the elements. Will we have to endure crazy rain like this? Will our rain gear keep us dry enough? Will weather make us miserable out there? Eventually I directed my thoughts away from fretting and surrendered to what will be.

As soon as I am up, every single movement has purpose to it. This morning's shampoo and shower will be my last for a while and, as I get ready, items are sorted into mountain luggage or luggage to be stored at the SENE office, my brain making a series of minute decisions. I pack my main writing notebook into luggage to be stored and from now on will use a small travel-sized one to record our time on the mountain. I decided a while back to use a framework of fill-in-the-blanks during our trek, anticipating I may not have cognitive energy to think about what to write each day.

Craig can fend for himself getting organized for the day. (Thank you, Sugar!) He and I follow the schedule set out for us: 5:15 breakfast, finish preparing our things, 6:15 meet at the cottage gate. We proceed through the schedule and now it's time for us five travelers to say good-bye and thanks to Abraham. Stepping through the gate, we are on our way to our prized objective, Mount Kilimanjaro.

Leaving the peaceful cottages we head on down the dirt path through the property, and meet up with Willie and the Land Rover. From last night's rains, the trail is squishy wet and I count it a win that I did not fall on the way to the pedestrian bridge. Under an overcast sky, we trekkers gather near the Rover and watch a team of porters coming down the path carrying our travel gear. I see my enormous hardshell suitcase resting casually on a porter's head, being gently supported with one hand as though the weight of it is of no significance. He seems oblivious, too, that the trail is muddy-slippery.

We watch as our things are passed up to waiting hands to be secured on the Rover's roof rack.

Ross is engaged with his good camera, capturing the moments. Craig, Sara, and Freddie take photos too. Me? I'm just being carried along with the unfolding of today's plan. I observe. I do what I'm told.

When everything is loaded we get in the Rover and begin
our way down the foothill slopes. We'd driven up this way from
the airport Friday night, through Moshi Town and Mbahe
Village, but this time we're seeing it in daylight. The narrow
village road cuts through a banana grove, and is lined with small
modest homes, some, mere steps away from the road, almost
like you can reach out and touch them from our vehicle. The
Rover rocks and sways over the rugged terrain. Numerous
children are making their way to school and skinny up to the
edges of the road in response to Willie's friendly beeping of the
horn, as though saying, "We're coming, please step to the side."
They are wearing neat uniforms and walk in small groups or
by themselves. I only see a few adults and it makes me think
this area must be safe for kids, that everyone knows everyone.
Frequently, those walking on the road will stop and wave at
our little group, like we are in a parade, calling out "*Jambo!*"

We are closer to the heart of Moshi and have graduated
to paved roads. Now, it's not the terrain keeping us slow, but
activity and traffic. There's a lot of movement on and alongside
the main road, motorized and people-powered, both. Many kids,
still, walking to school. The sky is dark and threatens rain but
no one seems worried about it; most are walking at an easy
pace. I continue to be drawn into the gentle invitation of this
culture to slow down, to turn down the mental dial of typical
American RUSH mode.

Sometime mid-morning Willie pulls up to the entrance
of a compound and stops in front of a tall gate. He beeps his
horn to announce our arrival at the SENE office. The gate is
opened for us and we enter an area, roughly half the size of a

football field, with its few scattered buildings, all of which is enclosed by a tall, private fence. We all are desperate to use the restroom, but there is just one. I pull the female, and age, card and go dancing on in.

Luggage is unloaded from the Rover's rooftop and sorted between what goes up the mountain and what remains behind. I have tons of cash, mostly to use for tipping the crew at the end of our expedition. Two women employees have Craig and me step into a small room, where my cash is recorded on a ledger and put into a large envelope, along with our passports and drivers licenses, which will be kept in a safe. All of our non-mountain luggage will be stored in this room too. I am uncomfortable parting with really important things, but force myself to trust this process. I keep a lonely hundred dollar bill aside to travel up the mountain with me. Just in case.

So here we are at SENE headquarters and I have not yet met the man in charge of all this, Simon Mtuy. When I was still on the hunt for a trekking company, and when the Colorado-based safari experts at the Wild Source gave me his name, I'd scoured the World Wide Web for information about Simon and his company. The wealth of information I found was like reading about a superhero, and his life credentials could fill a book. One of the many amazing things about Simon is he holds the record for the fastest unaided climb to the top of Kilimanjaro and back.

When everyone in our group is finished logging in valuables and storing surplus luggage, we are led to an exterior door of an office. The door is wide open and when he sees us, Simon stands up from his desk.

"Oh my God," I smack Craig's arm, "That's Simon!" to which my son rewards me with an eye roll.

With a huge smile he greets each of us, "*Jambo! Karibou!*"

He is boyishly handsome and has smooth dark skin. Above the desk, a fancy bike hangs upside down from the rustic ceiling. It would be easy to mistake this office for one in some small mountain town back home. The flags I brought from Boulder's Rotary Club had already been given to Simon earlier and, towering over me at well over six feet, he thanks me for them. He says he'll make sure to give me a flag from his Marangu Rotary at the end of our trek to take back to Colorado. Rotary Clubs can be found all over the place and are made up of community members trying make the world a better place.

I lean over and whisper to Craig, "This is fun… being a part of an international exchange of flags and uniting two clubs across the globe from each other."

While staff handle a few more logistics, Simon walks us over to a some short sections of hollowed out logs laying on the ground, and describes how they're used for harvesting bees. Nearby, there are a few chickens pluck plucking inside a small fenced enclosure. Pretty cool, at the headquarters of Simon's various business operations, the thread of active farm life is carried out.

We load up into the Rover again, and Willie continues driving through Moshi. We passengers are quiet but feasting our eyes on all the activity on the streets, a constant motion of people everywhere going about their day. Women are wrapped in colorful fabrics, in long flow-y skirts and head wraps. Men are mostly dressed in casual jeans and shirts. It feels like a different kind of busy — people are out and about and have places to go, things to do, but absent is the stressed look of people running around at top speed. Besides cars, vans, and trucks, the streets are full with scooters, motorcycles, bikes, many doubled or tripled up with other riders. Lots of food and merchandise is being moved about and being hauled in whatever creative manner possible. Footpaths and gravel shoulders lining the streets are active with pedestrians.

We turn into a thriving shopping area and transportation hub. Willie parks and we step out to stretch our legs and to use the public restrooms. The toilets are the most primitive I've seen so far and I have to figure out how to position myself over a drain hole in the center of the concrete floor in my stall. It'd be helpful to have a friendly little stick figure illustration. Which way am I supposed to face?

Gathered again in our vehicle, our group spends several minutes waiting. Before too long our head guide appears.

"Hi Tim!"

"Hi all," he says, with a wave, before turning to Willie to discuss business in their native Swahili. Then he climbs into the Rover, sitting in the far back between Sara and Freddie, his feet stretched out and relaxed in the aisle between the middle seats where Craig and I are sitting. Almost at once he is asleep.

We are moving again. The sky remains dark and overcast, but over the course of the day Willie has only used the windshield wipers a handful of times. Slowly we gain altitude as we leave Moshi and work our way to Kilimanjaro National Park (I call it The Park). We strain to look in the direction of Mount Kilimanjaro but cloud cover prevents us from seeing its snowy top. Town energy shifts to a slower rural pace. We see people shepherding goats or cattle, sometimes right up to the edge of the road, or sometimes crossing it. At times, it's as though we're the ones driving through the middle of their space, cutting through their pastures.

We stop at a small gateway village, swarming with people and activity; it feels similar to a farmers market, and looks to be a last-stop kind of place for those about to enter the wilderness of The Park. Tim gets out and is off somewhere presumably conducting business —gathering his crew? — while the rest of us wait. Tim comes back, talks Swahili with Willie through the driver's side window, and leaves again. More waiting. He comes back. It feels like there is a delay with the porters, my opinion. We trekkers simply wait and observe. Finally Tim is back again and crawls to the far back seat of the Rover, between Sara and Freddie. We continue our drive. Tim continues his nap.

The road begins a noticeable climb and pavement turns into a wide gravel lane. It isn't overly rough travel, but I am weary from being in transport for several hours. We pass miles of rich farmland, stretched out in all directions. Once in a while we can see workers in the field, way out yonder, and we eventually figure out they are harvesting carrots by hand. At last we drive into Londorossi Gate, one of the official entrances of The Park. Many large and medium-sized buses and many utility vehicles fill up a huge parking area, laden with porters, trekkers and all manner of equipment for the mountain. It feels wonderful when Willie turns off the ignition and we get to step out of the confines of the Land Rover.

A bus full of our crew arrives as well and in the commotion of the scene we trekkers are introduced to some of them. Not possible, but I wish I could stamp their names and faces immediately into memory. I'd say a couple of hundred people are milling about, our crew blending in with the other crews. In general, dark skin sets apart the Tanzanian guides and porters among pale-skinned tourists, mainly Americans and Europeans. Excitement buzzes: we are at the doorstep of grand adventure.

Tim tells us to sign in, pointing me toward a small building with about ten trekkers lined up outside of it. On the wide window ledge is a clipboard with sheets of lined paper where every trekker has to sign in and fill out several spaces: Names, passport numbers (we have passport pictures on our phones), ages, guide company, name of our head guide, country of residence. Inside, a park ranger patiently supervises the process. While we five are signing in, porters are setting up lunch in a large, covered picnic area, complete with tablecloths, napkins and reusable plastic plates. The feeling continues, the one I'd had since Willie picked us up at KIA last Friday—the joy of jelly-fishing and trusting in whichever way the current takes me.

The porters sort the tremendous amounts of gear they will carry and get in line so it can be weighed on a large free-standing scale. Except for the daypacks we'll have while trekking, the crew will haul our sleeping bags and duffles (and their own as well), along with tents, food, cooking equipment; tables and chairs for the dining tent; propane tanks, and the water filtration system. Also, the very important toilet tent.

Speaking of toilets and things pertaining to nature calls … preparing for this trip I was trying to work out in my mind how best to tackle going to the bathroom while on this expedition. SENE's packing list suggests, for men, a "urine bottle (for use at night in your tent)," and for women, "consider using a feminine urination device such as Freshette or GoGirl." So, a few weeks ago, I trail-tested the Freshette. You can use it without having to pull down half your clothing below the waist, and it can be used standing up if it's not in your physical wheelhouse to squat.

The device is a small bathtub-shaped cup that's placed up against the body between the legs and has a small tube for directing urine out and away from the body, much like the way guys direct urine away from their bodies. For me though, the little ministrations needed to use the thing canceled out its benefits. It was time consuming to remove the item from my backpack, then remove it from the ziplock bag I kept it in, and then attach, with absolute accuracy, one gizmo to another (the tube thing to the cup thing). An error here could result in having warm liquid streaming down the inside of your pants instead of out and away. Then the two parts had to be separated again to fit back inside the ziplock bag. And how do you keep it clean? And how do you keep your hands clean?

That said, I think it would be great for some adventures, like if you wanted to overnight in a hammock on the side of a cliff or something like that.

In my miles of hiking experience, when I step off trail for a nature call, I've learned to squat as low as possible to reduce any splatter effect. And I find a place near a big rock or tree branch which helps get me back up to standing afterwards, like how you'd use a handicap grab bar. For women still in child-bearing years, it's probably a good idea to plan a trip up Kilimanjaro around your monthly cycle. You don't need the extra discomfort that comes with having your period.

We finish lunch and return to the Land Rover. Although we are itching to get started on foot, we're not quite to the trailhead yet. Willie backtracks down the road we came up on, and before long turns onto a narrower road, ruttier and all around pretty adventurous. The road climbs. At one point there's a section blocked off due to deep mud and we are diverted around it, on the high shoulder of the road. A recent newsletter from our guide company encouraged travelers to ease up on expectations when visiting here, that things may not always go as planned. It's suggested to not worry, *hakuna matata,* you'll get to where you need to go eventually. It's helpful advice, slurping along on this road, as I wonder if we'll have a delay and for how long, but then adjusting perspective and remembering it doesn't matter. Willie is calm at the wheel as we crawl through impressive amounts of mud, ruts and potholes.

Finally, he pulls up where the road ends in a wide muddy cul-de-sac at the Lemosho trailhead. We step out of the vehicle as though released from the tether of civilization and my heart beats faster as we become fully immersed in this extraordinary place. It is less crowded at this trailhead, but there is still significant activity. A handful of other buses and utility vehicles have brought in crew and trekkers of other companies. Porters are busy organizing equipment. Trekkers are milling about waiting for further instructions. Nervousness, excitement, and the anticipation of our first steps on the mountain dominate my thoughts.

We wait for our porters bus before we begin trekking. After a while a few porters show up, on foot. Their bus is stuck, and Willie drives back down the road to see if he can help. Many minutes pass. We trekkers set up among picnic tables under a large roof and the language barrier means we know little of what's going on. Willie returns and waits, idling in the Land Rover, yet when he gets ready to leave, the gears won't cooperate and the Rover refuses to move. Now Willie is stuck too.

After more waiting, apparently all of our porters have reached the trailhead, having had to offload all the gear and abandon the bus a ways down the road. Waiting may have been inconvenient for our little group of five but we did manage to avoid the hassle of walking the slippery slide-y road up to the trailhead. The guides round us up to get started and one of them takes a collection of cell phone pictures for us in front of a large, noble sign. It marks the Lemosho route and indicates the elevation, vegetation zone, cumulative distance between camps and approximate hiking time needed to get all the way to the top, to Uhuru Peak.

Kilimanjaro National Park
Lemosho Gate
Elevation: 2100M amsl
Vegetation Zone: Montane Forest
From Lemosho Gate To:
Mti Mkubma Camp: 7KM (4 HRS)
Shira I Camp: 14KM (9 HRS)
Shira II Camp: 24KM (13 HRS)
Moir Hut: 34KM (17 HRS)
Barranco Camp: 34KM (19 HRS)
Karanga Camp: 39KM (23 HRS)
Barafu Camp: 43KM (27 HRS)
Uhuru Peak: 48KM (34 HRS)

Our elevation is roughly 7800 feet. It is quarter to four in the afternoon, twelve hours since rousing from our morning alarm. At last, after posing for pictures, we take our first steps on the mountain.

"Craig, this is it! Are you ready?"

He is all smiles.

Straight off, there's traffic-jamming as porters try to hurry on past us, needing to set up tents and start evening meals before trekkers arrive at camp. On the more narrow parts of the trail they have to be patient getting around us. As we follow the path through the forest I flux between needing a jacket or not, depending on shade or sun; the weather is ideal for a nice hike. Someone spots a blue monkey. It's in heavy foliage and hard to see, still, seeing a monkey in the wild is fantastic, and is a first for me (Craig's first sighting had been during a trip to Panama with his dad).

Porters heading to our first camp. Photo by Ross.

I think of Ali and how she'd be wanting to take photos of everything. She has a creative eye behind the camera and is especially good capturing nature. In 2010, when she'd graduated high school in Texas, I gifted her with a road trip through one of the most beautiful places in the world: Colorado. It was a difficult trip to plan because how do you narrow down all there is to see in the space of ten days? We began in Boulder and did a day hike up to Rocky Mountain National Park. Alison was ready with her good Nikon camera, having carefully charged it the night before. On the trail to Emerald Lake we saw snow! In June! She was only able to take a few photos and got very frustrated because somehow the camera hadn't charged properly. Before too long she got over her disappointment and we had a great time. After Boulder and Rocky Mountain, we went on to white water rafting and horseback riding near Salida in the middle of the state. We wrapped up our trip in the southwest corner of the state, in Durango and Mesa Verde National Park. On the drive home through New Mexico we stopped to get Alien beer for her dad. Because, you know, what a cool name for a beer.

Further along we are rewarded with a small group of colobus monkeys. Further still, a larger group is right off the trail from where we can clearly see them high up in the trees. Colobus monkeys are predominately black but with long strands of fluffy white fur. We stop for a few minutes and watch them doing their monkey thing, jumping from tree branch to tree branch, about twenty feet above us. An adult one takes a running jump from a high branch of one tree to the branch of another. Sara about has a heart attack as a little one comes following along, preparing to make the same jump. We are all in suspense watching it climb high, seemingly making

a plan how best to jump. It lunges toward the adult on the
neighboring tree, paws sprawled out wide. It lands on the tip
of a branch, and clings to it through a few big bounces before
scurrying toward thicker branches. So fun to watch.

"Alright," says Tim. "Let's keep moving."

We continue easy hiking up through gorgeous forest and
in my imagination I picture we're surrounded by some vast
invisible troop of monkeys. In reality, maybe I'm not far off
base... how many jungle creatures, hanging out high above us
in the branches, really are watching our every move? Maybe
watching to see if we inadvertently drop a snack or two. Since
entering The Park we've been steeped in green lushness of
rainforest, this particular ecological zone set at six thousand
to nine thousand feet. Of the five zones we'll trek, this one is
most abundant with life — plants, birds, and animals.

In the early evening we approach Mti Mkubma Camp.
Because it's hard to pronounce, it's just known as Big Tree,
and it sits at an altitude of 8700 feet. We follow Tim through
numerous clusters of tents of other climbing groups, in general
set apart by colors. It's an enormous campsite and set in a
relatively flat area of... big trees. We come to the camp's ranger
hut, where, same as at Londorossi, we are required to sign in
on a ledger. Evidently, The Park keeps detailed records of its
climbers. Then we trudge over to the camp sign, footed in an
enormous square of concrete and approximately twelve feet
high, the same style as Londorossi and Lemosho, and we strike
a pose for pictures.

An enthusiastic porter approaches me and calls out "Mama!"
He takes my backpack and gestures for me and Craig to follow
him, meandering through camp for a little ways and stopping

at three orange and white sleeping tents that are for us trekkers.
He shows which one is for Craig and me, our sleeping bags and
duffles have already been placed inside. He then points out the
gray dining tent a few steps away and, in another direction, the
gray toilet tent. We get the visual lowdown of our group's camp
in all of ten seconds. The toilet tent is set apart a little from our
personal tents, however, it's in the middle of this large camp-
ground and for an awkward half second I feel embarrassed about
how someone may see me going in.

I am very thankful for the porter assigned to toilet tent
duty. SENE's travel material says they line the container, what
would be the toilet bowl at home, with heavy plastic WagBags
from Cleanwaste, designed for human waste. It somehow gets
packed up and carried, from camp to camp to camp, and not
disposed of until we're off the mountain. (Later, I wondered
if there was something in place to allow for resupplying and
unloading of certain things for the crew further into the week,
but I don't know.)

We have been up and on the go since before sunrise but
now we relax, taking time to get settled into camp. Soon, we
are invited to gather in the dining tent for snacks and hot tea.
The overall vibe among us is excitement. Our adventure is
happening! Our little group doesn't linger over tea too long,
and after a short while Craig and I find out way back inside
our tent. With this bit of free time I scribble a few notes in my
journal, filling in today's blanks with the camp name, elevation,
and a few other items. I puff up certain parts that I don't want
to forget, like the little monkey performance in the trees. Craig
is relaxing, half way inside his sleeping bag, next to me.

"Mom," he says, "I thought we were going to just be driving for a couple of hours to get started at the Londorossi gate today." He looks at me, annoyed, as though I had something to do with this. "But nooo...."

"It took a long time to get started, didn't it?" I respond, not at all annoyed.

"It was nuts," he says, "We drove through that town, we ate lunch at the first weigh-in place," he keeps going, "and then the porters' bus breaks down and we had to wait for them before we could even start on the trail."

"I know," I shake my head. "What a day."

Called again to the dining tent for dinner, Tim passes around the oximeter and asks each of us about our water intake and other requisite questions.

He asks, "Everything okay?" We all nod. Hooray, our group is doing well. It's all recorded on our individual sheets: oxygen level, amount of water, how we feel, if we have a head-ache or any physical issue, if we're eating well.

The crew assigned to us this week is comprised of guides, porters and cooks. Tim is our senior guide and trip leader, and will work with two junior guides, Frederick and John. These three will always be with us on the trail. Tim coordinates with the head porter, who's in charge of the group of porters who do most of the heavy lifting. They're tasked with carrying the tremendous amount of gear, and setting up and breaking down camp. The head chef, Godlisten, manages several assistant cooks and is responsible for our meals.

When the health sheets are completed for all of us, Emmanuel, a young food server, brings us huge platters of food with a full-on friendly smile, going back and forth between here and the cook tent. The pattern continues … Godlisten provides as superb a meal on the mountain as Leonardo did in the foothills. I rate it five-star. The whole team is awesome. I can tell this is a smooth-running operation and that we're in excellent hands.

Before heading back to our tents for the night, we top off our water bottles from a large bucket of filtered water set in the corner of the dining tent and linger outside for a while, taking in the amazing rainforest that envelopes us. Near where our small grouping of tents are set up, is a very large group of trekkers making a lot of celebratory noises. They are in a large circle, whooping, singing and laughing. We see a flag on a long staff, the size of one you would see leading a band or a parade. We determine it's the Swedish flag. What are they all about? Do they intend to carry that enormous flag all the way? I mutter to Craig that I wouldn't want to be near them during a lightening storm.

As darkness of night encroaches, Craig and I prepare for our first night on Mount Kilimanjaro. We settle into our sleeping bags.

"G'night, Hon."

"Good night, Mom."

"Love you."

"Love you too."

CHAPTER 6

Elephant Spine

Tuesday, day two on the mountain.

I wake to the sound of a grown man giggling. Ugh, it's too early for this, not yet daylight. There is total silence and then it's interrupted by muffled giggles. It's someone in the big group of Swedes being egged on. Dang. After a few minutes of being irritated, it occurs to me it's better to wake up to giggling than to crying.

Our first night on the mountain was amazing. I slept with my sleeping bag fully zipped up with the hood part loosely cinched around my head. I had purchased our sleeping bags last summer for the sole purpose of using them for this trek. It feels a little silly to say, but now and again, over the past few months, Craig and I had practiced sleeping in them on the floors of our bedrooms so that when we were here we'd be familiar with them.

There's a soft tap on the canvas of our tent. Someone whispers, "Hello, good morning." It's Emmanuel, our server from last night. "Would you like coffee?"

"Oh my, yes please."

He proceeds to serve us from a thermos, two cups of coffee. We simply reach forward through the opening of the tent and *voila!* We don't even leave our sleeping bags. He brought cocoa powder and sugar too.

"*Asante!*" we say.

The cup of coffee sure hits the spot and I'm ready to take on the toilet tent. It isn't fancy, but it's better than wandering off into the jungle and digging a hole in the ground, and perhaps being eaten by a lion. The tent is tall, the size and shape of a single port-a-potty like you'd see at an outdoor public event. Stepping inside, and careful to keep my balance, I semi-straddle the seat as I manage underwear, lightweight leggings, and my hiking pants. There's about a foot-wide space on the sides and front of the seat. All cozy. On a positive note, it is good to have an actual toilet seat to sit on and not have to hover over an open hole. A roll of toilet paper is inside a small sling hung from the tent wall behind the seat, useful for hundred eighty degree back stretches.

I finish up with that and head to the dining tent for breakfast. Placed outside its entrance are basins of water and soap. Hand hygiene is essential for any expedition to prevent stomach troubles and ensuing misery; it's not an option to cut corners with this. Plus, my small bottle of hand sanitizer will have a permanent home in my pants pocket while we're on the mountain. We five gather around two small rectangular tables, shoved together, and draped with a colorful plastic tablecloth. There is room enough to sit, but not fully stand, inside the tent. Thermoses of coffee and hot water for tea are set before us and if something empties, Emmanuel brings more. He's tall, appears to be in his twenties, and has a generous smile.

John, maybe about Craig's age, is our guide *du jour*. He's already established a reputation of singing soothing gospel songs while out on the trail. Our three guides will rotate who'll be leading for the day, and always, the other two will be at the back of the line keeping track of everyone. It happened years ago, but I'd read that after summiting, a trekker went off trail to short-cut back to camp and he still has not been found. I think of John and how weird it would be to work on the mountain, away from your family for days at a time, often in challenging situations and with strange, bizarre tourists from all over the world. Oh, to hear some of their stories ....

The morning routine continues with John recording our oxygen levels, how we slept, how much we drank, and how we are feeling, did Craig and I take our Diamox. Altitude problems can be squirrel-y and it's tough to predict how someone will be affected by it. Sometimes, high altitude can affect the same individual differently at different times. We just won't really know whether taking Diamox will help us adjust better overall.

Emmanuel starts bringing in large platters of sliced fruit and we pass them around, family-style. Slices of pineapple, apples, oranges, mangoes, bananas. I am not a big fruit eater but this is the most fresh, amazing fruit. Next, platters of eggs, bacon and toast are brought in, Emmanuel keeping busy shuffling between the cook and dining tents. There is a type of porridge, which helps me stay warm, and very thin, crepe-like, pancakes that I cannot tell if they are a type of egg or bread. Butter, salt and pepper, jelly, honey, brown sugar, and cocoa allow us to doctor up our food and drinks to our liking. It is too good.

Breakfast winds up. "Okay," John says. "Today the trail leads us up and out of rainforest. It's not too hard and we'll just take it slow." Craig and I are happy and excited—we all are —and the trail doesn't sound too intimidating yet. "Get your things ready and we'll meet back here in a few minutes."

Back in our tent, we finish rolling up our sleeping gear which includes sleeping bags and thin flannel liners used inside the bags for extra warmth, inflatable pads, inflatable pillows, and shove it all into enormous thick plastic bags that SENE provides. I'd read about someone's experience of ending up with a wet sleeping bag because the porters hadn't kept it dry. Per his advice I'd brought along heavy-duty garbage bags just in case, but, yay, they won't be necessary. We pack up our duffles with our eight day's worth of our toiletries and clothing, and leave them next to our sleeping gear in the tent, ready for our crew who'll be hauling all of it for us. We stuff our backpacks with essentials we'll want for the day—two full bottles of water each, rain gear and snacks. I am cold natured so I am sure to put extra clothing in mine.

Our group is ready and we fall in behind John, the pace nice and easy. Within minutes, we pass out of the Big Tree campsite and the trail starts its upward climb. There are many other trekking groups of various sizes, trekking at various paces; some pass us, while we also pass others.

But the busyness gives way the further from camp we get. We see the huge group of Swedes, carrying their large country flag and I marvel at the thought of them carrying it the whole way up the mountain.

I nudge Craig, "Hey, what's their deal?"

"I don't know, Mom."

"Maybe they're a national sports team? Are they celebrating something?"

Craig shrugs.

Many of the porters convey an attitude of "the fun has begun!" Singing, smiling, whistling and "*Jambo!*" swirl around us. Some porters carry over-sized equipment, mysteriously hidden under canvas, on their heads. Others have large packs on their backs, always several, never just one, strapped together in any creative way necessary. Moving with agility and strength they pass by, high-tailing it to the next camp to set up. Aside from our three guides and a few other porters, I am not able to discern which crew is ours among the different guide companies blending and overlapping each other.

The mood on the trail is not serene and solitary; instead tons of people are out here in the middle of this huge mountain. By mid-morning, the last bit of rainforest gives way, the massive trees that felt inescapable earlier, make a shift to shorter ones. Transitioning to a heather and moorland zone, this portion of the trail is between nine thousand and thirteen thousand feet. I am loving this. Experiencing new things, my lungs and legs feel strong, my son is right behind me. Ali is near too, in my thoughts. What a beautiful day.

John stops at a relatively flat, open area where we have a grand view in the direction of Moshi Town far below us. It feels similar to being in the foothills outside of Denver and looking east across the Colorado plains. I find a big rock to sit on, pull out my water bottle and hunt around in my backpack for an energy bar. After a few moments, I wander off toward some tall scrubby trees to find a secluded spot for a nature break. Over the course of hiking a lot back home, I started the habit of lining my underwear with a panty liner, so when stepping off trail to go number one, it'd keep the crotch of my undies dry (I could never be bothered with packing toilet paper). It's a small detail that makes things more comfortable while on a hike.

I join the others gathered near the large rocks just off the trail. Along come some trekkers, *pole pole,* taking their time. Soon some porters come by. A few of them make a point to acknowledge us, calling out *Jambo!* I take a video with my phone to capture their greetings, whistling, and singing.

Over and over, one of them sings, "na na na NA NA!" He turns completely around in the middle of walking, fully performing for us.

Craig calls out a friendly, "What's up?"

He mimics Craig exactly, saying, "What's up?" right back, and moves his arms up and down like an athlete trying to excite a crowd. We all crack up laughing.

Behind him, another porter emerges from the vegetation and has a large load balanced on his head. As he strolls on by it's like he's on stage too. He opens his arms wide, as in Look Ma No Hands and greets us with a smile, "*Jambo!*" It's like watching a playful parade, with the porters entertaining us with laughter and silliness.

Hiking again, we keep going up, sometimes at a significant incline, and John keeps us at a comfortable pace. The vistas are so great. At times, looking up a slope, way far away, what looks like a small line of ants, we can make out teeny tiny images of other trekkers. We have to really look to see them through tall scrub. Colorful pinpoint dots bobbing along.

Clouds and mist visiting Elephant Spine. Photo by Ross.

After being on the trail for hours, one of the guides points to a long ridge up ahead. "That's called Elephant Spine," he says. "We'll follow the trail up and up, and it'll eventually take us along that ridge."

The smaller trees along the trail fade into short scrub and heather. John says the various little wildflowers we see are called everlastings, and even though they look so delicate they can tolerate harsh conditions. Afternoon clouds hide the tallest ridges in the distance but as we finally crest the Spine we look down and see across a huge caldera. It's a collapsed volcanic crater, eight miles long, and we will spend the next two days crossing it.

Descending from Elephant Spine, we close in on Shira 1 Camp, at 11,500 feet. Surrounded by magnificent ridges circling the plateau, it doesn't seem to me like we are this high. Light to moderate rain begins to fall, but we're wearing decent rain gear, so it doesn't dampen the playful mood. However, it does spur John to get us into camp as quickly as possible. He has us hopping to different paralleling segments of the trail, seeking higher ground where water isn't pooling as much. For the most part we avoid getting our feet soaked. I am warm except for my hands, but my lightweight gloves aren't waterproof so it doesn't make sense to put them on.

In camp, after signing in at the ranger hut, we have our photos taken at the camp sign, smiling, albeit looking a little soggy. We had hiked about five miles and gained over twenty-seven hundred feet in elevation. It's only day two, but I am eager to stick to the advice of taking things slow, drinking lots and eating well.

The same porter from yesterday approaches. "Hi Mama!" he says, reaching to help me with my backpack.

"What's your name?" I ask.

"Gusto."

I smile, "*Asante*, Gusto, thank you for taking care of us."

Sara, overhearing him calling me Mama, says, "That is so sweet!"

Having now crowned me with an affectionate nickname, Gusto leads Craig and me to our tent. For the record, I am the only mama in the group.

Other than the wet conditions, this place is like being in the middle of west Texas, desolate and without much visual interest. I normally have a good sense of direction but standing in the middle of this caldera, under cloud cover, I don't know which way our ultimate destination is, Kibo peak. Kibo is the tallest of the three volcanic peaks of Kilimanjaro.

Many other camps are already set up and it strikes me as odd, again, to think that in such a big place, on the side of a huge mountain, we are not alone out here whatsoever. While I normally seek solitude on trails back home, it doesn't bother me at all that the camps and trails are so active and I'm enjoying being a part of the culture of the Tanzanian crews on the mountain, along with the international flair of travelers from other countries. Wildlife used to be rich in this area and, years ago, guides regularly toted rifles for protection. But over time animals have moved out and have given way to trekkers. It's disappointing we shouldn't expect to see big wildlife, such as lions, elephants, leopards, and buffalo, but at least I'm not worried about becoming some creature's meal. So far, we have seen birds and monkeys, back in the forest. Here in camp, I only see large, well-fed, white necked ravens.

In our tent, Craig and I get our things organized. We unfurl and inflate our sleeping pads, about fifteen breaths worth, and roll out our sleeping bags.

"Hey, how's it going?" I ask.

"Good. The trail was easy," he says.

"It was a bit of a challenge for me." I'm rummaging through my duffle bag for a change of clothes. "I think it's cuz we're getting into higher elevation."

We wash up a little using the bowls of warm water and soap Emmanuel placed outside our tent a few minutes ago.

"It's fun," he says.

"Yes, definitely."

We've been given some time to take it easy and rest. Resting, my favorite kind of advice, happens to be good for acclimatizing. After a bit we go to the dining tent for afternoon tea. There's a big bowl of popcorn for all of us to share, but I'm not too thrilled there's not a better way to serve ourselves other than everybody's hands just scooping out popcorn from one big dish. Germ party! I don't eat too much of it.

After tea time we trekkers disperse. I'm pretty wiped out and don't have energy to explore camp, so I retreat to our tent. I tuck my legs inside my sleeping bag to keep warm and take in these sweet moments of leisure. Craig is back in the tent too, reading Ernest Cline's Ready Player One.

We are called for dinner. Inside the dining tent, the oximeter is passed around and John records our numbers. As we ascend over the course of this week, how altitude affects us and how it's dealt with, has everything to do with succeeding or failing to summit.

Emmanuel serves us and while we're eating, John looks at everyone and asks, "What is the reason you are on this trip?"

Straight away, Craig says, "In order to summit."

He goes on to tell about some other outdoor adventures we've been on and how this trek is a continuum of that, a natural process of doing a bigger challenge than the one before. Like, how it was a ladder-rung progression rafting in West Virginia and then the Grand Canyon. Same with skiing. The kids started out in southern Indiana when we'd lived in that region, but after we moved to Texas we started going to the snowy mountains of Colorado. The transition was easy.

I nod, "That's a fair way to explain how we got here."

Ross shares a little about how he ended up here and has a super interesting travel background.

"Wow," I say. "If you ever write a book about your adventures, I'll be the first in line to buy it."

Sara and Freddie add how they'd discussed Kilimanjaro with him and decided to join him in doing this. I'm shocked when Freddie admits he's really only here because of the big safari they have planned for afterwards. We five all seem to be decent travelers and I'm feeling comfortable about spending the next several days with our new friends. We're pretty much finished eating but continue to sit around; we have no where to go and nothing to do. Several kinds of tea, cocoa powder and hot thermoses of water grace the center of the table. Sara leans forward and takes a packet of peppermint tea. After letting it steep for a few minutes she says it's the best tea she's ever tasted.

"This is awesome!" she says.

It'd be fun to have Ali with us hanging out in the dining tent because she's funny and can tell a good story (not that I'd wish that kind of a life for her, but she could do stand up comedy). She made the right choice in turning this trek down. She does a little bit of camping with friends, but mainly steers from physically demanding trips. And, she loves books. She has so many books in her bedroom, it's like Poe's *Cask of Amontillado* —one day her bookshelves will close in and devour her. It works out just as well for Craig and me to be on this adventure and for Ali to be in her mental-adventures at home.

My son and I had been treated to a sweet insider's tip while on our Inca trek to Machu Picchu. In Peru, because summers are their rainy season, we had signed up to travel there during the winter. Nights on the trail in the Andes Mountains were crispy cold, and in the evenings before bedtime, they would fill our Nalgene water bottles with boiling water so we could cuddle up with them in our sleeping bags. So now, before we turn in for the night, I hold up an empty bottle and ask Emmanuel, "Would you please fill this with boiling water?"

Craig says, "Mine too, please."

Sara's eyes get wide and asks for that too. She turns to me, "Thanks for bringing that to the table!"

I believe Freddie was on board with this as well, but don't know about Ross, whether he deems it necessary to curl up with a hot water bottle. He looks pretty tough and gives the impression of being able to bear cold nights, you know, something like what Wim Hof might do.

My inner princess would not be happy if I froze at night on the mountain. Even the thought of being cold while trying to sleep makes me miserable. So, I'm grateful for Emmanuel filling my bottle with boiling hot water. And I'm grateful for the fancy sleeping bags I purchased for Craig and me. We had carefully researched what type of bags we'd need to get us through subfreezing temperatures. Maybe not tonight, but soon enough, we'll have frosty temps. We found some beautiful down bags by Marmot, a quality brand noted for their nice outdoor gear. After tucking myself deep inside my bag, I figured out the drawcord of the hood part and cinched it up snug around my head leaving only my little freckled face exposed to the air. Here, on our second night in this mountain wilderness, we are cozy in our tent, snuggled in our sleeping bags, with hot water bottles and inflatable pillows.

Yes, pillows. I know… we're not exactly roughing it. I bought inflatable pillows about a month back and had planned to put one under the Christmas tree for Craig. But when we had to make a couple of last minute runs to REI, he'd invariably end up in the camping aisle, and among other things, inspecting pillows. I'd yelled at him in the store that he was ruining my surprise.

"Craig, I hope you like your pillow."

"You're the best, Mom."

We both turn off our headlamps and I place mine in my improvised nightstand, my inverted hiking hat, inches away.

"*La la salaam.*" Good night.

"Good night. Love you."

CHAPTER 7

Dreams Traveled

Wednesday, day three on the mountain.

I wake up with happy anticipation. Hiking over the past two days has been a significant, but not over-arching, challenge. It feels good to be feeling good. In addition to just feeling good, one of the reasons for doing this trek is getting to spend large chunks of time outdoors, a means of escape from demands of civilized life — no responsibilities, no errands, no TV, no internet. Being out here radically changes my perspective of time. I'm not really concerned about it; I don't feel controlled by it. Out here on the Lemosho route, my day is simplified, narrowed down to two objectives, to keep walking and stay warm enough. These are my two tasks today.

Skies are clear this morning and since stepping out of our tents at daybreak, we have had gorgeous views of Kilimanjaro with its pristine streaks of white snow draped down its sides, like icing on a Bundt cake. After a hearty breakfast, we are packed up and ready to go. It's Frederick's turn to guide today. He's the largest guide, at a good six feet, sort of a gentle-giant type and, like Tim and John, has reserved mannerisms. All three of our guides carry enormous packs, I presume with emergency first aid equipment and other necessities we trekkers may need.

Frederick leads us out of the campsite and we step-stone across a small stream. He politely offers his hand to help me across. This is still the moorland zone, with scrub-like vegetation, but as we move higher the variety of plants differ a little from yesterday. There are rocks everywhere. Mostly they vary between the sizes of cars to bowling balls, on down. The trail itself is gravely and sandy smoothish through the rocky landscape, having been tromped upon by a kazillion tourists over the years. On occasion, we see building-sized boulders that must have tumbled down from some great volcanic event, looking like they don't quite fit in with the general landscape.

We stop for a break. "Craig," I say. "I had a bad dream last night."

"Yeah? What?"

"It was about our last day in Africa, when we go on safari," I say. "I dreamed that as the safari was getting started it turned out to be fake. It turned out to be a Disney tour with a movie-staged safari instead of the real thing."

"Sounds awful," Craig says, shaking his head.

"I was so upset. It was not what we'd signed up for!"

We had had a great time, when James and I took the kids to Disney World about twenty years ago. And, during the years we lived in Northern Kentucky, we practically wore out our season passes to go to world class amusements parks not too far away in Ohio. I have nothing against those things, it's just that our family has graduated to Nature's playgrounds. We have grown to especially adore Colorado where the mountains are just waiting for us to come play.

In 2014, I moved from Texas to Colorado after my twenty-four year old marriage fizzled and died. My relationship with James, the love we had for each other, had slipped away, year by year. Like a boiled frog that'd started out in comfortable water, it became too far gone to bring life back into it.

In the summer of 2015, Craig moved to Colorado, into one of the upstairs bedrooms of my new home, after his first year at the University of Arkansas didn't work out. He was in a searching mode and unsure what direction to go with his education. Later still, in the summer of 2016, Ali came to Colorado after graduating from Texas Woman's University with a degree in Psychology. She's upstairs in the third bedroom now, but had started out living in the basement so she and her two cats could have lots of space. (One cat has since moved out of state with a friend; the other moved to kitty heaven.)

Yes, I am their Mom, but my kids would not have followed me if I'd moved to just anywhere. The mountains were a major appeal for both of them. Since moving to a beautiful area near Denver, they've cycled through living with me in my comfortable, modest home, venturing out on their own, returning home, out again, and back again. It works out splendidly. Spending the past few years exploring Colorado's trails and slopes, has given me and the kids a better understanding of, and more respect for, challenges that come with extreme mountainous terrain, weather and altitude. It's an advantage for us now as Craig and I make our way up Kilimanjaro. Plus, we have inflatable pillows to help get us through the night.

We continue trekking, making our way to Shira ll Camp across the wide Shira Plateau, the trail taking us gently up. Temperatures are cool, making for perfect weather, and as we make our way, clouds creep in and the sky darkens but we do not encounter rain. However, Frederick has a large red golf umbrella strapped onto the side of his pack.

My shoulders start to complain a bit, feeling the weight of my water bottles in my backpack, so I clasp my hands behind my back to alleviate its weight (looking cool and casual). I have happy feet, knees and hips though. Craig doesn't appear to be having any issues, as there's no grumbling emanating from his direction. He's just calm and (really does look) cool. Other than my shoulders, the trekking is going well. Our little group of five is getting to know each other better and it seems we keep circling back to the topic of travel and other experiences we've had. New travel ideas lead to the delightful burden of wondering which places to explore next.

My Travel Dreams list is fluid. Dreams are added or deleted; some have been traveled. Through having moved a handful of times when we were still an intact family of four, and through traveling for fun, we've been to many different states, including Hawaii and Alaska. Once to Canada and a handful of times to Mexico.

With one or both kids, I've taken them to Belize, London, Yellowstone (with Ali and in the heart of winter: Fabulous), regularly to Breckenridge, but (with Craig) have tried out the slopes at Taos and Jackson Hole too. The Inca Trail. And, like getting off a roller coaster, Let's do it again! I knew immediately after our family rafted through the Grand Canyon the first time, that I wanted to do it again. So eight years later, Craig and I returned for another one hundred magnificent river miles.

With one or both kids, James has taken them to Thailand, Dubai, the Peruvian Amazon, Honduras (where they all learned to scuba dive), and (Ali) Egypt, and (Craig) Panama and Costa Rica.

Alison has traveled with friends, mainly in or near Colorado; and California.

Craig has traveled with friends around Colorado too. Also Paris and southern France, Amsterdam, Belgium, Barcelona and Baja California.

Now, Kilimanjaro. Mother and son.

We continue across the immense plateau, *pole pole,* working our way up to 12,750 feet. I ask Frederick about a weird looking tree I notice for the first time. He says it's a giant groundsel. It's about twenty feet tall and is similar to the shape of a cactus, its trunk splaying upward into thick fingers, which are topped off with large green leaves. Here and there, I begin to notice others.

My breathing is coming on pretty heavily so talking is minimal and my thoughts start to wander off on their own. What's everyone else doing out here? It's beautiful and glorious, and also harsh and uncomfortable. What am I doing here? This feels like an act of defiance; climbing Kilimanjaro is a little crazy, a little uncomfortable. For the most part though, I'm here because it satisfies my itch to be immersed in beauty for several days.

Getting ready for this trip, four obstacles stood out to me as my biggest challenges. Things that pushed my Comfort levels.

First, I do not like to fly. I will fly, but I don't like to. I'd have to accept the long flights getting to Africa and back. It's hard for me to sit on an airplane and not move for hours at a time.

Second, cold weather. I'd have to prepare for several cold nights on the mountain, arctic weather on the summit, and the possibility of trekking in rain or snow.

Third, I anticipate I may not sleep well. Being in a tent is not the same as being in my own bed, and high altitude effects sleep as well.

Fourth, the difficulty of the trek itself. Factoring in Kilimanjaro's high elevation, there's significant risk of altitude sickness. Besides that, all kinds of things can sabotage summiting. Not everyone gets to the top. Some people die.

At the moment, hiking along, I am feeling great and am so enjoying this spectacular place.

Following along behind our guide, our quiet group moves through this empty, rocky landscape, one step at a time. During occasional stops, we find rocks to sit on and rummage through our daypacks for a snack. Or, to catch up on breathing, adjust clothing, answer nature's call, take pictures. We all take in hearty quantities of water. While on pause with trekking we also get to watch the steady stream of animated activity marching on

From left to right: Sara, Freddie, Guides Tim and John, Craig, and Guide Frederick, and me. Photo by Ross.

by, other trekkers and the many crew who make their living on the mountain.

We have hiked a pleasant five and a half miles, and by afternoon arrive at Shira II Camp. The Machame route converges here and there's an uptick in the amount of people. We know the drill, and after signing in at the ranger hut, taking pictures at the camp sign, we proceed on over to where our tents are set up.

Relieving me of my backpack, Gusto greets me, "Hi Mama!"

"Hi Gusto!" I like his friendly energy, "how are you?"

He leads Craig and me to our tent. As I plop down inside the tent, but with my feet still outside, I start fumbling to remove my gaiters. But Gusto insists on taking them off for me and then helps me take off my muddy hiking boots as well. There's no better way to feel like a queen. Craig and I relax inside our tent, getting ourselves organized a little. I am tired. I'm tired from hiking in high altitude, but also because I'd slept poorly. I have a bit of a scratchy throat but it's no big deal.

"So far," I say to Craig. "You and I are proving to be a fine pair of mountaineers." I inflate my sleeping pad and lay out my sleeping bag on top of it. "We're not dealing with stomach issues, blisters, headaches…." I remove my outer jacket and plop back on top of my fluffy sleeping bag.

"I'm wiped out," he says. "But wouldn't want to miss any of this."

"I'm super tired," I close my eyes. I'm bushed, but my hiking stamina is holding up well and I only notice being tired when we're stopped.

I have no energy, so laying flat out in the tent feels amazing. The past few months have felt like a race against time setting up this trip as best we could. But since landing in Africa everything has been delightful and hanging out in camp is pure relaxation. This campsite is flat and rocky, similar to our previous camp, and we're still in the middle of the open expanse of the caldera. The temperature is fairly cool, but there's not much wind. After resting for a while we are called to the dining tent for snacks and there's hot tea and cocoa if we want. I go for some hot cocoa to warm up and then we go back to our own tent again.

I tuck myself half way into my sleeping bag. I look at Craig, "I'm warm, yay!"

"That's good, Mom." He grabs his book out of his duffle. "It's been another really good day."

"So cool that we're doing this," I pull out my journal and pen. "Seriously, I would not be out here if it weren't for you wanting to do this."

It is true. If not for Craig, I would not have taken on Kilimanjaro. He mentioned it to me on the Inca Trail and I happened to capture it on a list and happened to give it more thought years later. And so happened, too, reasons to go outweighed reasons not to go. But it all started with him.

"And here we are," Craig says, laughing a little.

After a decent rest we're called back to the dining tent. We top off our water bottles from the large bucket set in the corner, keeping one empty so Emmanuel can add boiling water to it later. Routine health questions are asked. Sara is the hydration champion.

"You down an entire bottle of water more than I do." I look at her and shake my head.

In reply she holds up her water bottle like a trophy.

The oximeter gets passed around; with it, we're all looking for high readings, somewhere in the range of 95% or higher for oxygen saturation. Among us, a few altitude symptoms are creeping in, nausea and headaches. But they are minor. Emmanuel ducks into the tent bringing steaming platters of food. I am thrilled with how good the food is coming out of the cook tent.

"Emmanuel, this is so good," I say.

Guide Frederick nods, "We never get complaints about Godlisten's cooking."

We five seem to be holding up well. Our conversation centers around how the day was for everyone. Eating with Ross, Sara and Freddie, whom we've known for half a week, reminds me that group travel is part of the adventure too, strangers thrown in with strangers who've never met. My simple hope, when signing up for this trek, was to avoid being teamed up with someone hard to get along with. Like, The Over-bearer, who never steps back and lets others offer a comment or opinion. Or The Complainer. Or The Toxic Family. What a way to stink up an epic trip. Sort of like, even if you don't smoke, but if you're in the same room with someone who does, it still stinks.

Back in our tent and getting ready for lights out, I cinch up the hood of my sleeping bag even tighter than last night. The flannel sleeping bag liners we have inside our bags are touted as giving us an additional twenty-five degrees of warmth. Maybe that's true. I'm wearing a decent amount of clothing and I'm wrapped around my hot water bottle too. Yay, I am warm enough.

"Craig, can you believe there are twenty-five crew helping us up the mountain?" I interrupt his reading.

"Are you serious?"

"Yeah, the guides and porters and cooks." I'm lying in my sleeping bag, eyes closed.

"That's intense," Craig says. "Twenty-five to us five… that's five to one."

"Have you heard about KPAP?" I say.

"What's that?" Craig gets fully into his sleeping bag too.

"The Kilimanjaro Porters Assistance Project," I say. "They see to it that the men and women working on the mountain have adequate food and clothing. And fair wages."

"How do you know all this stuff?"

"I found out about it when I researched this trip. It made me want to be sure to pick a company that treated their workers well." Whether the weight of their loads were correctly recorded and if they were eating enough, I had no way of knowing, but it did look like our porters had decent footwear and clothing. Our three guides, who we're spending most of our time with, have good boots, gaiters and rain gear.

Craig says, "The porters all seem really nice." He turns off his headlamp.

"I agree."

The mountain trails are crawling with trekkers and we all need a great deal of support. The crews are the glue that hold everything together. I feel well taken care of, and it feels genuine too that we *mzungu*, foreigners, are welcomed here. I hope our presence is a good thing for the gracious people who make their living on Kilimanjaro.

Alright, let's see if I can sleep tonight. *La la salaam*, goodnight, day three.

"Goodnight, Sweet."

"Goodnight, Mom."

After a minute, "Mom, I think Gusto has a crush on you."

"Haha! You're so funny!"

CHAPTER 8

Lunch Above
Fifteen Thousand

Thursday, day four on the mountain.

What is the best possible way to wake up at 12,750 feet? Emmanuel is gently tapping the outside of our tent and hands me a cup of coffee, candied up with cocoa powder and sugar, and then hands Craig's just black. With or without caffeine, we're excited for today's trek. The highest altitude he and I have so far achieved had been 13,828 feet at Dead Woman's Pass in the Andes. In a few hours we will hike as high as 15,230.

"Craig," I say. "This is so easy. We just have to wake up and Emmanuel brings coffee."

I have established a personal MO of getting up once in the middle of the night for the toilet tent and what I notice, in this coffee moment, is my bladder isn't overly uncomfortable when I first wake up.

"And someone's making breakfast for us…"

"I think the trip preparation is harder than the trip," I say.

"Mom, you did all the planning."

"Yeah, but still," I look at him. "You had a part in it. You had to be in really good shape."

I'd spent the past several months gathering supplies for this trip, capturing essential details and getting my body in top physical shape. One reason this trip seemed attainable to us is Craig and I both have a steady habit of working out. Playing soccer as a kid, swimming as a teen, and keeping up a gym habit as an adult, Craig ended up the epitome of a sexy lifeguard at Lifetime Fitness. Oh wait, he *was* the sexy lifeguard at Lifetime Fitness. He no longer guards or swims, but has kept up the gym habit. Physically, he can do anything he wants to.

My fitness routines started years before Craig was born. My go-to habit is running because of the convenience of it. I put on running shoes and head out the front door (for many years the family dog made that non-negotiable). Although I've been a runner for over forty years, I consider it a filler activity, something I do on days I don't go to the pool.

Swimming is what I love to do. When I was a kid, summers were spent at our family cottage on a small lake where I played all day in the water. I was never an athlete or played team sports, instead, I simply liked to be outdoors. Later, as a young adult, I started a new kind of swimming—no longer in a lake, but by doing laps in a pool. Thus making my favorite outdoor activity a predominately indoor one.

Both of these things remain a part of my day to day. And now that I live in Colorado, hiking has been added to my repertoire.

I do not keep track of my workouts the way I did thirty, forty years ago. Working out is as routine as eating for me; it's not like I have to remind myself to do it. Yet, as soon as I booked this trip I started keeping records as a way to see I was keeping in good physical condition, and, something new, to push myself a little. I don't have a competitive personality, rather, my reasons for working out stem more from the sense of strength and well-being I get from it. I had fun though, with an adventure on the horizon, working toward a specific payoff for keeping in shape and Kilimanjaro became my (peak) motivation.

When I started "training" I was doing three types of activity every week. I was running two or three times (three to five miles), hiking once (in altitudes between six and twelve thousand feet), and swimming three times (at about fifty laps a pop, which is the equivalent of 2500 yards). All of it, aerobic. I did not micro-manage my workouts through health apps. I didn't track heart rate, steps, calories, or other minutiae. I just did my thing.

I wasn't tracking Craig's fitness preparation, but he's twenty-four and in great physical condition, most of which comes in the form of lifting weights. He is also good at making healthy food choices, an area I could use some improvement with, but am not sufficiently motivated to act on.

"What do you think you did to best prepare for this trip?" I ask. "What advice would you give to others?"

He considers for a moment, while he finishes getting dressed. "Uhhh, be in good shape?" Then he says, "I'd say too that having a bit more mental strength than usual helps on the trek… like knowing you're exhausted and still continuing… Don't expect it to be a walk in the park, and understand that you're going to be unpleasant for a few days."

"Yes, I totally agree," I say. "You gotta have the mental piece of it too."

Time to eat. Craig and I walk the few steps to the dining tent. Our guide today is John, the gospel singer. Someone asked him about it and he said singing gospel songs was a common way to pass the time for many porters on the mountain. Our vitals are taken and soon after Emmanuel steps into the tent bringing us another amazing breakfast, along with his cheerful smile.

"We're just going to go slow today, a little slower than usual," John tells us. "We're getting up into higher altitude so it may feel a bit more rough."

"Lava Tower today, right?" someone asks.

"Yes," John says. "It'll take us all morning to get there. That's where we will have lunch."

Excitement permeates… I think we're all looking forward to today. "Be sure to put rain gear in your backpacks," John adds, as breakfast finishes up.

Craig and I top off our water bottles and then take care of last minute chores — teeth-brushing, toilet-tenting, gear-packing. When we're ready we go stand near the others, waiting, with hiking poles in hand. Again, my two simple objectives are to keep walking and keep warm enough.

Departing camp, we start to ascend into clouds. The going at this altitude is especially *pole pole*. We are on a four hour stretch of continuous uphill and John sets a wonderfully easy pace, respectful of the effects altitude can have on us. For me, today is the first real physical challenge. I am feeling it. I am not by any means in distress, but I know I'm calling on my body to challenges not experienced before. My breathing is labored and the weight of water in my backpack has my shoulders complaining again.

During our rest breaks, after a moment to calm down my breathing, I play catch up on hydrating and take time to drink a good dose of water. There are two general ways to drink while hiking. Many people prefer a drinking system similar to the Camelbak hydration pack which gives you ready access to its water tube whenever you feel like it. This tube, in essence a large straw, attaches to a gizmo on the shoulder part of your backpack and allows you to drink from the bladder stored in your backpack. It's great to use if you want to drink en route and is super convenient.

However, I like to use a wide-mouth Nalgene water bottle instead. One reason is I find it difficult to drink while on the move, especially going up-trail, because of the greater effort to breathe, so having ready access to a drinking tube is unnecessary. Two, a significant downside to the CamelBak is that the tube will freeze in higher altitudes. You can expect that to happen on the final summit push to Kibo or anytime there are very cold temperatures out here on Kilimanjaro. I'd had a small-mouth water bottle freeze on me, at its opening, during a beautiful winter hike some time ago in Colorado, and it prevented me from being able to drink from it at all, which is the same as having no water. The bottle became permanently useless even for future hikes as the freezing caused the top of it to crack and it no longer sealed. A wide-mouth bottle will take much longer to freeze and so is a better option. I'm a fan of the Nalgene bottles for their wide-mouths, their indestructibility, and their ability to transform into luxurious hot water bottles.

The more we walk, the more into the clouds we go. Imagine: clouds we normally see that gather high in the sky, when we'd normally be standing, lifting our heads to look up at them—

we are up there, that high, quite literally walking into them. In my mind, snowcapped Kibo peak, our prized destination, majestically rises to our left. All morning though it hides from us, shy behind cloud cover. Our landscape today is defined as alpine moorland and I feel like we're on a different planet. There are rocks everywhere, many covered in lichen, among grasses and heather. Most of the vegetation hugs close to the ground. There are no trees. Dark gray clouds shroud and surround us.

Our small group trudges forward and up, and except for an occasional comment, we are silent within a kind of beautiful solitude. The guides are bringing us to Lava Tower, an unusual geologic edifice known as a volcanic plug, at an altitude of just over 15,000 feet. A long time ago lava shot up through a vent in the mountain and cooled in the form of a tower. Although we hike directly past this three hundred foot Tower, standing serene and spooky, we are in such thick mist, we can only see its base and a little ways up it.

This morning's trek is hard work, so I am glad when we get to the Lava Tower camp. John brings us into the campsite to our dining tent, set up and waiting for us. We only plan to stop for lunch and then we'll be getting back on trail. Rain starts, making noisy splattering music on the canvas tent. We five trekkers look a bit wiped out, a little scruffy, yet I sense low current adrenalin humming among us. A kind of giddiness.

"Has anyone been this high on a mountain before?" John asks. He has to talk loud over the sound of the rain.

We all shake our heads no.

Here we are, eating great food, sheltered in a big tent, at 15,230 feet. During our meal the sound of the rain gets more intense. Our trip itinerary points out that on a clear day there are three hundred sixty degree views from Lava Tower, including views of a dramatic gap called the Western Breach that'd been formed by lava some time ago. We are not privy to these views today, but it's still spectacular being here. Climbing routes which have included the Breach used to be popular, but in recent history deadly rockfalls have diminished its appeal. SENE, and other companies too, no longer offer it as an option, but it serves as a reminder this mountain is rough and rugged.

After eating and marveling over our extraordinary altitude, we take time to put on as much rain gear as possible because great buckets in the sky have been upended. Our canvas tent is a worthy barrier protecting us and we are encased in a safe little place with impressive turmoil just outside of it. Until we are ready to step out of it, that is.

The initial descent from the tower is steep and immediately I'm using all I've got to pay attention to my steps, careful to place my trekking poles just so. I dedicate my focus to remaining upright and not on my butt, my brain in overdrive to avoid falling. Any kind of a slip could lead to an ankle injury, and any kind of little injury, actually, could hinder my quest for the top. Somehow Tarzan — I mean Ross — is able to navigate this tricky, super slippery terrain, *and* take some photos.

I am thrilled Ross is in our group because he's been taking pictures with a nice camera. He sometimes gets ahead of our group on the trail, or gets some other perspective. It takes additional energy while we're hiking, and while we're in camp, for him to do this. I don't enjoy taking pictures. I would rather be on a hike, surrounded by scenery and wildlife without a camera to interrupt the moment. Plus, I often feel capturing something picture-worthy falls short and doesn't adequately

Descending Lava Tower. Photo by Ross.

convey the fullness of what I've experienced. Craig and I are taking a few photos with our phones, but the good camera we had packed remains ignored.

"We could sure use Ali as a photographer out here," I say to Craig. The walls in our home are graced with photos Alison had taken on previous trips. "But I wonder if Ross would be willing to share some of his photos with us."

Pretty quickly, the steepness of the trail tapers to a gentle slope. Down-hiking just a few hundred feet brought us out of the rain too and we're back into mist. I'm no longer working so hard to not fall.

I come up alongside Tim. "I expected to see more signs of litter on the trails," I say. "Especially on a such a busy mountain." This part of the trail widens and a small group of trekkers pass us. I really had expected that we'd see food wrappings and plastic water bottles once in a while.

"Kilimanjaro is strict on litter. All of the groups out here have to pack out everything," Tim says.

We walk along, side by side. It is still gray, but we can see better and it's one of the prettiest places on the mountain so far. It is fairy-tale like, an oasis of sorts.

"I appreciate not having to walk through other people's trash," I say. "It keeps the beauty of the place pure." We pass by streams and small waterfalls, no doubt running full due to today's rain.

"Porters have to weigh their gear at the entrances of the mountain and it gets weighed again at the exit gates." What Tim is describing is Leave No Trace principles, which the Kilimanjaro National Park operates under. Everything packed into The Park must be packed out. He helps me navigate a steep area, waiting for me to get around a few large boulders. "And crews work during the off season to maintain trails and pick up litter."

Further on, we walk through groves of exotic giant groundsels, the cactus-shaped trees we'd seen earlier. They are grouped here and there, and although tall, we are not enclosed by them. Scattered around are shorter plants, called lobelias, that remind me of pineapples because of their coarse, pointy skin. The foliage is whimsical and it feels like we're in a children's picture book.

"I can tell this place gets taken care of. It looks really good," I say. "The entire time we've been out here it's been so beautiful."

"Thank you," Tim says.

Our group pauses to take a few pictures and remove rain gear. Craig and I had gotten sturdy ponchos for this trip and

Giant groundsels. Photo by Ross.

they've kept us, and our backpacks, desert-dry. Others in the group wore rain jackets and used waterproof covers for their backpacks.

Craig is stowing away his poncho. He says, "We ate lunch at fifteen thousand feet…" Straightening, he murmurs, "But now we're hiking down to … what's the elevation at our next camp?"

"Somewhere around thirteen thousand," I say.

"Weird to think we're going down to thirteen," he says.

It is serious business paying attention to how best adapt to these sustained altitudes. We're playing the hike high/sleep low card, and along with that, the *pole pole* card. The leading cause of failing to summit is developing a severe form of acute mountain sickness (AMS). A handful of trekkers do die on the mountain each year and the main culprit is the effect of altitude. We are halfway through our expedition and will be in serious altitude, this high and higher, for another three full days. Not until our last night on the mountain will we be back inside friendlier oxygen levels.

For two more hours we have an easy trek through gorgeous Barranco Valley. I'm feeling the altitude a little with my energy running low. There's intermittent light rain. We're walking in an area where an immense landslide has carved out the valley, almost a thousand feet deep in places, many many years ago. My soul wants to inhale this beautiful volcanic gloriousness.

CHAPTER 9

Dental Drama

We arrive at Barranco Camp. Rain hinders visibility, but it's apparent this area was formed by a huge landslide and the visual drama is intense. What a treasure to see this. At 13,077 feet, this campsite sits on a wide swath of land, surrounded on three sides by immense walls standing guard over it. Relative to these walls our campsite tents are like the size of cars surrounded by New York City skyscrapers. We sign in at the ranger hut and strike a pose in front of the camp sign. It continues to rain, the clouds apparently enjoying our company, having followed us from Lava. It is cold. How cold? I don't know. I must not be too miserable because I offer a big happy smile for our group picture. Of our group, I am the only one wearing (lightweight) gloves.

A narrow ravine separates this camp from the Barranco Wall, where the route will take us tomorrow. On the opposite side, at the far end of camp, there is a small group of buildings, a tall post with a windsock, and what looks to be a spot for a helicopter landing. It's hard to find consistent information but, loosely, there are about a thousand rescues on the mountain each year. This is a trekkers statistic and doesn't include guides or porters working on the mountain. Just because our particular group has been doing fine does not mean others are not without troubles. Seeing the windsock reminds me that our "doing fine" is not something to be taken for granted.

We had hiked up for four hours, then down for two, and I am physically spent, yet, except for my weary shoulders, I feel great. I don't have any niggling aches—no headache, no nausea, no feet problems such as blisters or bloody toenails. My knees and hips feel fine. My tooth is fine. With a large array of possible problems on the mountain, the SENE suggestions for first aid items to pack seemed enough to supply a field hospital. Still, I had packed an assortment of things: aspirin, ankle wraps, Tums, moleskin and blister care, etc. If you have a problem it'd be handy to be able to fix it. It's a packing conundrum though. How do you prepare for the unexpected and how do you decide you've packed enough?

"Thank you, Gusto," My shoulders are relieved when he takes my backpack although it's no longer weighted with full water bottles.

"*Karibou*, you're welcome," he says. We follow him to our tent.

Craig nor I are super talkative people on a normal day, and now after such a long day, we are quiet and simply content with taking in our surroundings. I think Craig is feeling good. And probably real tired. We make our tent all cozy, then gather with the others in the dining tent for snacks and hot drinks. It feels like a social experiment, grouped together with strangers while on an adventure, because we're unadorned by the typical stuff we're surrounded by back in civilization. Our true, unadulterated personalities can't hide behind fancy clothes or big houses. Our careers and degrees don't matter too much out here.

The rain has chilled me. When I raise my cup to sip some hot tea my hand shakes so much, I have to set it down right away to avoid sloshing it all over the place. Our group is circled up at the table; all of us are pretty quiet and energy is running low.

Our guide asks, "So how did you all end up here?" We'd had conversations about this earlier, but the topic picks up again.

Craig says, "Any type of family vacation we'd taken in the past usually involved something beyond simply sight-seeing. We like outdoor stuff."

"We've traveled to big cities too," I say, "But mostly we like to do something active."

Sara and Freddie share some of their experiences, but Ross stands out from the rest of us when he talks about some of the extreme adventures he's done, putting him in a whole different category altogether.

As we're talking I eventually thaw enough to be able to sip my drink. "I feel lucky to be here. I just got over having a problem with a tooth." I point to the back of my left jaw. "A tooth started bothering me a little, like three months ago. Then it kept getting more annoying."

As this trip loomed closer my tooth issue loomed larger. I wasn't sure if it was my tooth, jaw or my ear causing the trouble, but when I hiked in higher elevations and really cold temperatures, it would cause a deep ache to set in. December came about and I was busy with the extra demands of the Christmas season, busy finalizing details for this trip, and then busy with this particular issue.

"Here comes my tooth, interrupting everything and demanding my attention," I drink more from my cup. I'm warm now.

It was an ordeal. I went to the dentist, then a specialist, but ended up back at the dentist again, all the while working around their restricted holiday hours and pleading for appointments ASAP. I had to have it resolved before Africa.

"Mom was getting worried," says Craig.

"My dentist removed the tooth the day after Christmas and I was so happy to get on with my life. Everything was okay."

Until it wasn't.

"But a few days after the tooth was removed, the ache returned. Just a little at first, but then it got worse," I say.

My anxiety ramped up. I began to fear I may need to CANCEL this trip. I called my dentist again but couldn't get in touch with him because it was the week of New Year's and the office was closed. Africa was a week and a half away.

"But after that, it got better on its own, right?" Craig stands and starts gathering plates and cups together so they can be cleared.

"Yes, thank God!" I stand too. "It was crazy that such a little thing almost caused the trip to fold." Emmanuel comes in to clear the table. "I think there may have been an infection at the root area and that it simply took a few days to heal even after the tooth came out. It feels great to be able to be here with all of you."

We all start leaving the dining tent. "We're glad you could make the trip!" Sara says.

Siesta time comes next and I gladly take part, laying full out in my sleeping bag. I may have even closed my eyes a little. A while later we are again called to the dining tent for dinner.

Circled up, health checks are recorded by Tim. There are no alarming oximeter readings among us and only a few minor physical complaints. The simple fact that everyone shows up for dinner is a clue that we are fine, fine enough anyway. Each day, with each new level of altitude, we are more vulnerable to problems. In general, there's a seventy-five percent success rate getting to the summit. On longer trails, such as the one we're on, the success rate skews higher. Our guides continue to urge us to have plenty to eat and drink, and to take advantage of resting while in camp.

We continue to hang out around the dining table, most of us nursing hot drinks, after another fabulous meal. Roughing it, luxuriously. Tim has some goofy riddles no one is able to understand. The atmosphere inside the tent feels awkward, a little off base, like a blind date gone wrong. We're laughing a lot though, as we struggle over gaps of silence. Our quiet, reserved group would have welcomed someone like Trevor Noah or Kristin Wiig to step in and loosen things up. At one point Tim takes out his phone, eliciting oohs and aahs, as he proudly shows us pictures of his one year old son. I offer to show pictures of my son too, pulling up photos on my phone, of the big kid sitting next to me (isn't he CUTE!). Tim looks confused at first and then bursts out laughing.

Given that this is the second week of January, I ask Tim, "Are we the first group you've guided this year?"

"No" he says, "I led another group already. They wanted to be on the summit to ring in the New Year." He goes on, "The mountain had about four hundred people summiting that day — for New Year's and for the new decade, 2020," explaining that people didn't merely want to be on the mountain for New Year's but on its summit.

"No kidding?" I'm surprised.

"Really?" Ross says, "Four hundred summited on New Year's?"

"Yeah, it was crowded up there. People stood in line to get their pictures taken at the sign," he says, referring to the sign marking the highest point on Kilimanjaro. "They had to keep the line moving. So people would pose, have their picture taken and then move on to let the next group come up."

I try picturing a crowd lined up at 19,341 feet: pose, click … pose, click … pose, click …. This place is so interesting. Do I describe it as a unique experience or one that's common among mountain enthusiasts?

The skies clear up as we finish dinner. Earlier, someone had wondered if we'll get a chance to see the top of Kilimanjaro and Emmanuel, our food server, said yes, around 7:00 PM. Nearing that time now, seemingly right on cue, we step out of the dining tent and the beauty takes my breath away. Kibo's bright white mantel of snow, closer now, sits just above our camp. We see the Barranco Wall better too and I am mesmerized by it, a geologic work of art, rising almost eight hundred fifty feet high.

The air is crisp, and becomes colder as the sun sets, so I do not stay outside very long. It's time to turn in for the night. I brush my teeth and use the toilet tent. I confess, while planning this trip, I gave way too much headspace anticipating what to do about peeing in the middle of the night. I very much wanted to avoid having to get up in the night for the bathroom. It meant extracting myself from my sleeping bag, in the cold, in the dark, putting on hiking boots, freezing on the way to the toilet tent, then coming back to the tent, removing my boots … I'm exhausted thinking about it.

So, to try to work around this, I'd bought a box of the adult diapers, Depends, and a half dozen or so traveled to Africa with me. In the end, only two ended up in my duffle with me here at camp. However, I'd failed to rehearse what it'd be like to pee in an adult diaper inside my sleeping bag at night. Even a tiny mistake could mean a lingering smell of urine for the duration of the trek, so the Depends remain in my duffle, unused. Now, with four days worth of Kili-experience, I have a routine where I consume most of my water during the bulk of the day and taper off in the evenings. This means saying No to that enticing, hot cup of tea after dinner. I still am up once in the middle of the night, but only once, and it turns out, it hasn't been a big deal.

Another part of the human experience on this mountain is I am super tired because I'm not getting decent sleep and so I haven't been starting my days feeling fresh and restored. Add to that, hours of challenging physical activity. Add to that, altitude. Add to that, the times I've been cold (always while in camp when we're not doing the physical work of hiking).

But emotionally, I am having the time of my life. What a gift to be able to do this! I can't wait for the Wall tomorrow. It's the one hiking segment out of our whole week that requires scrambling, the use of both our hands and feet, to get up. Nicknamed the Breakfast Wall, it's usually climbed in the morning. After breakfast.

I am radical tonight and before switching off my headlamp I take two Advils, thinking it'll help me sleep. Of course, I am snuggling again with my hot Nalgene bottle, and it is pretty close to heaven-warm in my sleeping bag.

"Night, Craig. Love you."

"Night, Mom. Love you too."

La la salaam.

CHAPTER 10

Scrambling

Friday, day five on the mountain.

I had a great night's sleep, thanks to Advil. And, having gone to sleep with my Nalgene bottle filled with boiling water, by morning it's lost its heat and I drink down the whole liter before leaving my tent. In the pre-dawn light, when I stand up outside, the massive size of the wall is more apparent. The headlamps of the porters who're getting an early start are displayed as tiny bouncing pinpoints outlining a wiggly, vertical path. Then the pinpoints disappear somewhere along the top.

I have all morning to freely consume coffee, water and juice, and take full advantage of the toilet tent while in camp. I appreciate the porter who manages the toilet, who has it emptied and fresh for us each morning, who keeps a supply of toilet paper for us. We trekkers get health-checked and are served breakfast. After we get packed up for the day our group gathers near the guides.

"Tim, could you help me tie my trekking poles onto my backpack?" We need hands *and* feet for the wall this morning and poles will only get in the way.

"Here, give them to me," he says and he stows them with his things.

"Thanks!"

I'm ready for the Barranco Wall. Photo by Craig.

We have barely left camp when we descend a little and step-stone across a few easy streams, this pretty little ravine decked out in garden-of-Eden splendor. Frederick is leading us today, setting the pace, and I am next in line behind him.

Once across this narrow gorge we start to climb. It's intimidating at the start because I'm not sure what to expect. During our trip-prep phase, I found lots of entertaining comments about the Wall, online, ranging from people being terrified of it to those who were giddy-excited about it. For our group, it's turning out to be very doable and I feel like a kid on a huge playground.

"Craig, how do you even describe this wall?"

"Just that it's all rocks," he says.

I pause to glance down. I see Barranco camp across the ravine, and it appears now like the size of a LEGO play set, from the perspective of looking down from a ten-floor high-rise. The streams we'd crossed twenty minutes ago look like gray threads. Climbing, it feels something like going up an exterior fire-escape of a building, only, instead of stairs, we are scaling huge boulders and rocks of various sizes. Fantastic! At certain, more dicey areas, Frederick tells me exactly what hand and foot placement is best. I turn and give the same instructions to Craig behind me, then he turns and tells the person behind him. I am full of energy and feel like Spiderman, climbing and scrambling along higher and higher.

Kissing Rock is unexpected. All of a sudden, Frederick is showing me how to traverse, sideways, against a solid rock face. My arms out wide, my face within kissing distance from this rock, I have to shuffle my steps sideways on a rock shelf, bridging a chasm. This chasm looks like it simply drops off into oblivion and for a second my brain isn't sure how to instruct my feet how to maneuver. I'm surprised I don't remember reading about it, but Sara and her brother Freddie have a healthy fear of it and have been anticipating it. Freddie, especially, seems to have a very good grasp of the details of our entire itinerary. Throughout our trekking so far, it's as though he has encyclopedic knowledge of the mountain. Does he study Stedman's guidebook each night?

Safe on the other side I'm engrossed as I watch the others come across. With Craig though, my stomach flips when he takes his turn and I can't watch him. Guides Tim and John, bringing up the rear of our group, do not even give consideration to this gap and simply breeze across it. It is something else too, watching the porters, especially those with the heaviest, bulkiest equipment, stepping across as though it's a city sidewalk. I'm impressed how they patiently wait in line for trekkers to cross as well, because there's a bit of a back up at this spot.

The Kissing Rock. From left to right: Me, Sara, Freddie, Craig and Guide Tim. Photo by Ross.

We keep climbing, using hands and feet to hoist ourselves upward. Beyond Kissing Rock is one other "yikes" section, a huge smoothish boulder. Frederick turns and tells me how to approach and conquer. Once we have all scaled this part, we step off trail at a small outcrop for a short break. We take a moment to guzzle some water and watch as a constant line of porters, interspersed with trekkers, climb up this particular boulder. One porter, carrying something huge, all wrapped up with tarp, gets caught on part of an overhang and snags the top portion of his load. We see, for the first time, a porter stumble, his balance and strength no match for his top-heavy load. Several nearby porters immediately come in to help, all friendly and accommodating. After getting to a more stable spot, he loads up again with all his stuff and gets back to tackling the wall.

After an hour and a half, we reach the top of this behemoth. We rest, gulp water, recover our breath. This is my favorite part of our trek so far. I am exhilarated, and thrilled to be pushing myself to climb the biggest mountain on the African continent. Outwardly, I am sure I just look tired.

"Craig, ya hoo, we're doing this." I give him a side hug. He's doing a great job, and doesn't even look tired.

"Mom, this is so cool." We do a high-five.

Yesterday, Lava Tower was a super achievement. Today, Barranco Wall pushed me even more. Each day's hike is a little more challenging than the last and also becomes my new favorite. All of us climbers appear to be doing really well. Seems to me we are like-minded in having the time of our lives. Well, possibly, or is it that Freddie is just a really good sport, doing this in order to claim the prize of going on a safari afterwards? What I realize, sitting with our humble group during breaks, is

Almost to the top. From left to right: Sara, Tim, me, Freddie and Craig.
Photo by Ross.

that no one gripes or complains. I love that. I love our group.
It is wonderful not to bear the burden of discontent even if it's
not mine.

The views are magnificent even though, again, clouds
conceal Kibo. Looking onward, this part of the mountain is cut
with deep ridges down its side, as though King Kong dragged
its massive claws, from the top of the mountain down, through
the terrain, leaving ridges behind. Up on our present ridge, on
top of Barranco Wall, we see gorgeous Karanga Valley laid out
in front of us. From where we are now, we'll go down into the
valley, cross a significant stream at the bottom, and then make a
steep climb up to the next ridge over, accordion-like. Tim hands
me my hiking poles and we start on down. Going down is a
different kind of work than going up. It's easier to slide and
stumble on the gravely path. Add to that a set of tired legs, throw
in some especially steep places, and this section becomes
demanding. To help distribute my weight better, to ease the
impact on my knees, I place a lot of upper body weight on my

poles. This, though, causes my pectoral muscles, and all across the front of my shoulders, to become sore.

Up close, I can discern the trail beneath my feet for only a little way at a time before it disappears, as it serpentines through boulders, rough terrain and sparse vegetation. But while we're stopped for a water break, I notice tents that are a part of the next camp on the far ridge where we're headed. Looking over the valley, the trail on the distant ridge looks smooth as it climbs up from the valley floor, and appears to go directly, steeply, into our next camp. There's a second trail, not quite parallel to the main one, that leads from the camp high on the ridge to the stream below, intersecting it further upstream than where our path crosses it.

I take a moment to catch my breath. "Tim, what's that other trail for?"

"The porters use it to get to the stream. It's the last place for water until after we camp at Barafu Huts," he says.

"Oh," I say. "Oh yeah, now I can see there are people on that trail."

So, not just for our next camp, but also for our highest camp in two more nights, the stream running through Karanga valley is the last water source on the mountain, until we are on our way back down it again.

The more we descend, the more lush and numerous are beautiful exotic plants that hug close to the tumbling waters flowing through the valley. We become surrounded by more of the pretty, fantastical-looking lobelias and groundsels unique to this area. Getting closer to the stream crossing we more easily see the secondary trail and the porters on it. The ones going down, with empty buckets, are practically running due to the steep slope. The porters going up, carrying water, are moving slowly, using their hands to steady the five-gallon buckets on their heads. I looked it up — five gallons of water weighs 42.7 pounds. Wow.

The trail is packed with trekkers and crew as we approach the valley floor. With fewer camps on the upper reaches of Kilimanjaro, the main ascent trails serve to funnel and collect more people into them. All around us are wonderful African sights and sounds. Same as when we began our trek days ago, the porters and guides continue to be energetic, friendly, colorful, and often they wave or greet with the ubiquitous "*Jambo!*" Sometimes a porter from one group sees another porter they know in another group and, in passing, effortlessly chat about for a while, in their native tongue, not breaking stride as they hike. Then they disperse and merge with their own groups again.

There is much activity in the sky as well. All day we have been under, or in, clouds. Or above clouds. When a vista avails itself we see clouds all over the place, moving toward us maybe, or maybe cruising by in another direction. There is minimal sun, which is good, because we're not getting sunbaked out here. In the garden paradise of the valley floor we come to the flowing waters and cross over on large rocks laid out like a path through it.

We begin our climb up the second King Kong ridge, the one that's been in view since getting to the top of the Wall this morning. Frederick is so great to keep a slow pace and never are we urged to hurry. I am not sure if our group would be going faster if I weren't here. Wait, I know Ross is going slower than he is capable of. But the twenty-somethings are probably pretty satisfied at the pace, especially since, back in the States, Sara and Freddie live near sea level. Plus, Craig has told me a few times my pace has kept him from feeling overworked. Actually, it does not even matter and I think of my daily mantra: keep walking and keep warm enough. That's all I need to do today.

I am breathless when we step into camp, and overcome with wonder. The folds of the mountain trail today took us up a towering wall, down nine hundred feet to the valley floor and up a remaining three hundred feet, landing us in Karanga Camp. Our work yields a net gain of less than two hundred feet. Even so, this location has us high in the sky with an eagle-eye view of the world around us. At 13,250 feet, we're stationed on a rocky peninsula that slopes downward like an enormous finger from the body of the mountain. Far and away, weather can be seen—areas of blue sky, areas of clouds, areas of rain. Our porters have somehow managed to pitch our tents in a relatively flat space, some of the tent lines held down tight by big rocks. This campsite is similar in size to the others and features huge rocks, some as big as cars, some house-sized; and lots of enormous rock piles. Just beyond and above us, Kibo Peak, with its signature snow-topped bonnet, seems *right there,* and although still hidden by clouds, Uhuru, our ultimate summit point on Kibo, is undeniably close.

We sign in, smile for pictures at the camp sign and head to the dining tent. A nice surprise, we are served chicken pizza for lunch. All of our meals have been superb, but this feels like a touch of home. I am tired, happy and enjoying pizza. I feel encouraged. Each day, with harder physical demands, I have another layer of confidence that I'll achieve the summit. How cool to know that a steady habit of keeping fit over most of my life has allowed me the ability to do this. The mental piece Craig touched on earlier is as important as the physical piece. As we experienced new adventures, our mental "muscle" grew.

As with many things in life, our adventures had a ladder-rung pattern. Little by little, they kept growing. Our thirst for "more" kept growing. Often these trips came with a strong sense of not knowing what we were getting into, but our mind-set was we wouldn't know unless we tried. We just gotta go and see. With Kilimanjaro, we expected it to be hard, yet with a Let's Try, we give it our best shot. Right now, on the side of a super tall mountain, it is wonderful. We are having so much fun. I am elated for Craig and me pushing ourselves to the edges of adventure like this.

We are up in the elements of active weather. Clouds come and go, fluffy and white; at times, dark and menacing. They move above us and in and out of the valleys around and below us.

Craig and I, along with Sara, Freddie and Ross, wander around camp after lunch. There are several trekking groups scattered around. We mostly stay along the camp's perimeter, taking in indescribable views, and occasionally glimpsing Kibo if the clouds allow. We walk past our porters' tents. They have made themselves at home doing routine things of daily life, as though it's perfectly natural here above thirteen thousand feet. A few are doing chores, like washing personal clothing, socks, t-shirts and whatnot, and laying them out to dry on rocks. Out of the whole crew, there is one female porter and she is bent over large buckets cleaning up pots and dishes from lunch. Tim had told us that only in recent years have women been allowed to work on the mountain, and I've seen a few out on the trails, laden with gear just like all the male porters.

I wonder about the many tribal influences represented among the mountain crew. Earlier, during one of our meals, John had explained there was something like a hundred and twenty ethnic groups, and each group had their own language. Between groups however, Swahili was used to communicate. I think of having grown up in Michigan and moving to Texas in my twenties. What if Michigan had its own language, different from Texas? But we'd use, say, English, to communicate? In Tanzania, with each passing generation, John said the local dialect of a particular tribe fades because it gets pushed out in favor of Swahili. Young kids at home are growing up speaking less and less in their tribal tongue.

We move slowly through camp, taking our time. I'm bundled up against the wind. I'm loving the fascinating scenery, both the campsite we are in, what's right in front of us, and also the zoomed out setting we're in, looking out off the slopes of the mountain, miles out. We see several porters bringing water to their groups, stoic and soldier-straight. Carrying weighted buckets on their heads, having come up the long, steep trail from the stream, their usual animated expressions are now subdued.

Camp Karanga. Photo by Ross.

"How are you doing?" I ask Craig. "Everything okay?" We take a rest and sit on some boulders, along with the others.

"Yeah," he says. "This is great." He hands me my water from my backpack.

"How are your ankles?"

"They're good," he looks down and rotates one foot and then the other. "Yeah, they're doing good." He had broken both ankles at the same time back in high school, while being too rowdy at a local playground (stressful because we were only two months out before our Inca hike in Peru). Then he re-broke one of them a year later, almost to the day, while double-bouncing on a trampoline with a friend.

"That's really great to hear," I say. I give him back my water bottle to put away. We'd sought out good sturdy hiking boots for this trip, to keep his ankles stable and, fingers crossed, protect them from injury. Also, I had packed not one, but two, ankle braces as part of our mountain first aid kit.

"Yup, they seem be doing fine."

I'm proud of Craig. This morning he did great climbing up Barranco, and hiking the King Kong ridges to this camp. He still has an appetite and is eating well; he's tolerating the altitude. With him, there's little drama and everything is just fine. His ankles too.

We all get up and walk around some more, the five of us all in a good mood. We are proving capable. We are doing it! Despite being six thousand feet below the summit, it feels like we're already on the top of Africa. It's a one of a kind experience—we are standing on the ground, on earth, but given the windy conditions and active weather moving all around us, it feels more appropriate to say we are in the sky.

Walking around I keep an eye out for where our route will lead us upward tomorrow, but we are in a world of rocks, an enormous field of massive volcanic boulders and I can't find any discernible trail. I've become cold, so I creep back into the tent to keep out of the elements. It's too cold to use the soap and small bowls of warm water that Emmanuel brings to our tent, but I have a packet of body wipes and use those for my hygiene needs. When Craig comes back to the tent he uses the small bowls of water to do a wee bit of laundry for socks and underwear. Like the porters do, he lays them out to dry on rocks.

Halfway in my sleeping bag, taking some time to relax, I grab my little notebook and pen. Unless I capture our days on paper, my memories will get fuzzy and I won't even remember which mountain we're climbing, let alone remember what happened on what day. I record a few fill-in-the-blanks for each day during our trek:

Best part

Toughest part

Weather

Altitude

Camp

What I learned from guides

My mood

Unexpected

How I slept

Me and Craig how we're doing

How I feel physically

Animals

Plants

Today I add, I just want to rest and relax and go about the business of acclimatizing.

I snooze a while; I feel lazy, pampered. Craig is nearby in his sleeping bag, perhaps taking a snooze as well. Time passes and we are summoned for dinner. Crawling out of our tent, clouds have opened up enough to display Kibo looming regally over the camp, cloaked in white. Simply. Breathtaking.

The oximeter gets passed around while Tim asks us the routine health questions.

"I heard people my age are more likely to summit than someone Craig's age." I place the oximeter on my index finger.

Tim nods, "Younger folks are apt to hurry to the top and they end up getting altitude sickness."

Tim's recording our numbers. I tell him my oxygen reading and how much I'd had to drink.

"That's the main reason I wanted to take this longer route. To give us time to acclimate. I watched someone on YouTube recording his climb out here and he'd gotten a super bad headache and had to turn back," I say.

Tim says, "But even if you do all the right things for altitude, there's still a crapshoot aspect. There's no guarantee you won't experience problems."

Emmanuel ducks into the tent with a platter of fresh fruit (still!) and we pass it around. He has such a great smile and keeps everyone happy. Soon, he brings us broth with vegetables in it. I take some, more for warmth than anything. Once the broth has been served, he returns with more platters of food and while we pass them around, Tim is keeping an eye on how much we eat. A few of us are prodded to eat more. I'm eating okay but my appetite is not robust.

"Tim," I say, "how is our group doing?"

"Good, real good," he says. What I see around me, all of us huddled together in the dining tent, two and a half miles into the sky, is that we're all present. Our group is functioning okay and showing up for meals. No one is laid up and refusing to get out of their sleeping bag. Several of us are dealing with mild altitude symptoms; mine basically is, I'm exhausted. But trekking at a slow pace and keeping well hydrated is guarding our group from more extreme issues. A great attitude permeates, an undercurrent of excitement for being in this extraordinary place. And Tim affirms that we are okay.

After eating, and with nothing else to do, we continue hanging out in the dining tent. Tim tries to entertain us again with more awkward riddles. When he tells us the answers we all sort of groan. Is it culture that makes them incomprehensible? Is Tim bad at telling riddles? Are these little cognitive tests to see how we're doing with altitude? Among us, Craig got one answer right, something about finding a zebra in a refrigerator.

"Okay," says Tim. "Tomorrow is our hike up to the highest camp."

Someone asks, "How hard will it be?"

"Not that hard…it's a short trek," he says. "Only three miles." He says the altitude will have us moving at a slow pace. We'll get to next camp and do a lot of resting, acclimatizing, above fifteen thousand. We have no more questions and we get up to vacate the tent. "Be sure to dress warm," Tim adds.

Dusk now, the five of us gather outside. We clearly see Moshi Town far below us, defined by its lights, beyond which there is only thick velvet blackness. It's such a crazy view from so high up. Craig and I are in awe, taking in the glorious scenery

— the drama of the sky, the clouds and weather. We watch an isolated storm, with purple-dark clouds and lightning flashing, as it moves across Moshi, far *below* us in the distance.

Today has been nothing short of spectacular. Back in our tent, we get ready for the night. I'm craving another night of decent sleep, wanting to overcome the heavy fatigue I have. I'm wearing several layers of clothes, am wrapped around my boiling hot Nalgene bottle, and have my sleeping bag as tightly cinched up around my face as possible. Just my little mouth and nose are peeking out.

A short while later, *la la salaam*.

"G'night, Craig. Love you."

"Night, Mom. Love you too"

CHAPTER 11

Higher

Saturday, day six on the mountain.

I wake up with happiness swirling around in my head, "Craig, we're doing it!" We're ready to take on another amazing day.

I'm glad Alison had decided to stay home. She would for sure love the massive beauty we've been trekking through all week but not so much the physical discomforts. Discomforts that are more challenging each day. Besides, she's already a Rock Star in her own right, having overcome significant challenges in her life, and doesn't need a physical mountain to know she is one tough woman. For many of us, achievements we've managed to reach may go unnoticed by others, but that doesn't mean they don't matter.

Emmanuel wakes us up with a tap tap on the side of the tent and hot coffee. I desperately need caffeine because of lack of decent sleep. I do not understand how spending days doing the hard work of trekking up and up, and up some more, does not translate into exhausted, blissful sleep at night. My happiness is tempered in that I'm facing the day already tired.

I had woken up feeling just this side of nauseous and with a slight headache, but everything clears after I drink down a liter of water before even being fully out of my sleeping bag. Somehow plain old water makes things okay. My morning camp routine seems to play out in slow motion. I make sure I am dressed for cold temperatures, head off to the toilet tent, then the dining tent; everything slow-mo and methodical. My body is not buzzing with energy, but proceeds, like on a slow fuse, from one task to the next. If I weren't using quite so much energy for my own personal needs, I would be more attentive and enjoying the activity taking place in camp around me.

After breakfast, I finish getting suited up. Craig and I meet up with the guides while we wait for everyone to gather. I am nervous about getting into harder territory. There's a mix of wanting something badly, but realizing it will be so tough. It feels similar to when I was well along in my pregnancy with Ali years ago. As a first time mom-to-be, I was excited but full of anxiety, facing the imminent approach of labor and delivery, wondering how hard that would be. Now, another day closer to the top of Africa's highest mountain, there are no options but to go forward. It'll be the hardest thing I've ever tried to do, and without the benefit of an epidural.

Everyone is ready and Frederick leads us out in comfortable *pole pole* style. Exiting Karanga, it's mountain rush hour with several other groups of trekkers getting their morning start, funneling up and out of camp. This is the start of the toughest two days of the trek, with today and tomorrow blurring together into one seriously long day. This morning we'll cover a little less than three miles to next camp, which will serve as a place for eating and resting before a midnight start for the summit, about sixteen hours from now. Our challenges go beyond the physical aspect of climbing a mountain, because although we will have opportunities to rest, we will be missing out getting a full night's sleep. I've never faced an endurance test like this.

Soon after we exit the campsite, the trail drops over a slight ridge and our surroundings open up into vast alpine desert. The terrain is desolate, with no sign of flora or fauna, save white necked ravens. All manner of volcanic rock still dominates, but this part of the mountain opens wide and presents us with grand, expansive views. We pass stacks of rocks that line the path here and there. Some are tall and linear, and other massive piles of rocks make up more of a conical shape. The trail is easy to see and we don't need the cairns to navigate, but I imagine they are absolutely necessary in bad weather. I think, too, that some rocks have been stacked by sentimental travelers wanting to memorialize that they've passed through. (The ethics of Leave No Trace would discourage doing this.) I'm curious about these cairns, curious about a lot of things actually, but I need all my breath to keep moving, so I don't ask questions. I don't want to exert myself more than I have to. I trudge, I breathe, I observe.

After a while the trail crests on a significant ridge and views seem to have no end. The path stretches before us, then begins a long descent into a shallow valley before climbing again to the next ridge. In general, there's a steady line of people on the trail, we *mzungu* filing along single-file, but at times spreading out in sporadic chunks. The porters fan out off the trail to pass different groups, carrying loads of gear to next camp, including water from Karanga, skirting over and around endless volcanic rocks. Before too long, Craig gets my attention and points up ahead. We can see our next camp high up on the farthest ridge. It looks miniature, like looking through binoculars from the wrong end. Pausing to take in the expanse, I realize I'm doing okay and let go of the nervousness I'd started the day with. There's a festive feeling in the air when trekkers from different groups pass. Like there's an awareness we're all in this together—facing the longest hours, the hardest hours, of our adventure.

It is cool and cloudy, with moderate wind. The windproof shell I have over my winter jacket keeps chilly, wispy tentacles from finding their way inside my clothing.

Crossing the shallow valley from Karanga to Barafu. Photo by Ross.

I try to be smart about how to dress for the weather; it creates a lot less drama. Not being able to summit comes down to problems with altitude for the most part, but other reasons for failing are related to injuries or not being prepared for mother nature. We've encountered rain this week, but sleet and snow is also possible, and if we can't keep warm and dry it'd be very tough to continue on. Way back during our first whitewater trip in West Virginia, our guide had informed us how "cotton kills." Cotton is comfortable to wear and feels great when it's hot, but when your shirt gets wet from the river, or if you're sweating a lot while trekking Kilimanjaro, that same shirt will make you cold, possibly hypothermic, when temperatures drop because it'll take forever to dry.

The ups and downs of today's terrain are slight. I slog along. I'm breathing hard, but I'm comfortable and staying warm. Trekking ever higher each day, there's much to be grateful for. Aside from my tired shoulders, Craig nor I have physical issues.

There've been no major headaches, no tooth problems, no dehydration, no severe fatigue, no knee, ankle or toe problems. As far as I know, not even a blister.

We get to an area below the next ridge, having spent all morning crossing the shallow valley. On a large, slightly sloping, mostly flat space, we stop. Lots of other groups have stopped too, like cars pulling off an interstate at a designated rest stop. Most of the day's trek is complete. Groups of people are sitting around looking out at the incredibly expansive views, re-fueling with snacks and water, regaining breath. Craig takes a short video. As he pans toward me he says, "Hi Mom." I look at him and my weary state of mind instantly switches. I flash a huge smile for the camera.

Soon, our guides have us up and moving again. The trail gets mean as the slope increases significantly, comparable to a blue ski run. It gets more narrow too and we merge into slow-moving, single file formation. Time feels suspended. The only real thing going on, for me at least, is that we continue hiking.

It feels amazing getting to Barafu Camp. We are 15,360 feet in the sky, higher than any mountain in the lower forty-eight. If you're wondering, Mount Whitney in the Sierra Nevada Mountains, comes in at 14,494 feet. There are three high altitude zones: High, Very High, and Extremely High. We have been in what's considered the Very High range, twelve thousand to eighteen thousand feet, since the third day of our trek, which occurred while crossing the Shira Plateau. For at least another twenty-four hours we'll be in this Very High range, touching briefly into Extremely High range when we summit, before we drop back below twelve thousand to a more hospitable atmosphere. Merely being here is a feat.

Waiting to sign in at Barafu Camp. Photo by Ross.

I'm glad we're in camp but it's still some distance to reach the sign-in hut. My energy running low, I would prefer not to have to hike a single step more than necessary. Finally, we come to the ranger hut. A few trekkers are in line ahead of us and while waiting to sign in, I try to take in the huge amount of activity all around.

I nudge Craig, "Feels like we're on a strange movie set." Camp is sprawled out along rough, inhospitable terrain on these upper reaches of the mountain. I hear foreign languages and accents. If it weren't for being exhausted, it'd be fun to hang out for a while to people-watch and observe everything going on. A mix of crew and trekkers, with all manner of clothing, gear and equipment, display a disheveled, multi-cultural scene. Different groupings of tents are in various stages of being set up.

Craig nods, "Yeah, it's kinda got a carnival vibe."

Faces portray a range of emotions, from full-on cheerful smiling to muted exhaustion. My stomach twists though, when I notice some trekkers look downright distressed, downright unhappy. But overall the mood seems to lean toward that of accomplishing something quite spectacular, I don't know, like a team facing the finals in a grand competition. I am so attune to the privilege of seeing this. To be here. To take part in this.

Barafu camp is one of three base camps on Kilimanjaro which accommodates trekkers before their last push for the summit, making this camp the size of a small village. I am curious about the other groups we see. What is their purpose? Where are they from? Are they competing, or maybe raising awareness for a particular cause? Or, like us, simply here for the experience? The Swedes that we've been criss-crossing paths with since our first day seem to have a mission. They are, after all, carrying their huge country flag all along the way.

Upslope of camp I see a line, like a pencil drawing, extending from camp and reaching as high as I can see up the peak. Eventually I notice tiny colored specks along this line, trekkers, moving in both directions, up and down the mountainside. We are close to the top yet those specks of color give me perspective —the summit is still a long way. After the five of us get signed in we walk over to the camp sign. The name, Barafu, means "ice." We are just below the arctic zone of the mountain, on Kibo peak, the tallest of Kilimanjaro's two remaining main peaks. We are aiming for Uhuru, Kibo's summit. The camp sign indicates the distance to Uhuru Peak is three miles. Yet, the estimated hiking time is seven hours.

Three miles at altitude is a whole different animal than three miles at sea level.

After our sign pictures, we weave in and around other groupings of tents, down a ways to where our particular camp is. I whine, internally, that our tents are down, that we are backtracking several feet and further away from the path that'll take us up later tonight. However, I'm not whining about the glorious view of Mawenzi, Kilimanjaro's other main peak, seven miles east.

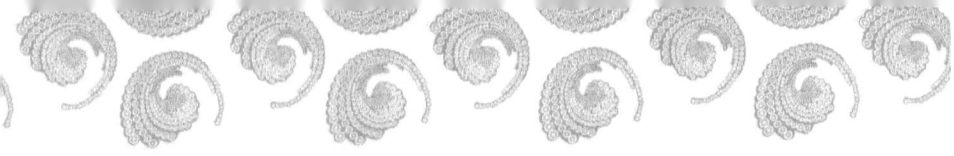

CHAPTER 12

Attitude

I t is quite an event walking in this camp. Once we step off the well-worn main path, we are walking on large flat slabs of broken rock, at significant slope. Where we normally think of the ground as being solid, here it is not. I have to walk gingerly as I am walking on layers and layers of various sizes of volcanic rocks. With my physical fatigue and a little issue with coordination, I'm sure due to altitude, the ground feels like it undulates, like I'm traversing a rope bridge.

I feel dopey. Fatigue is kicking my butt. When we are shown our tent I collapse inside. Craig appears less stupefied than me. We remove our boots and take off our backpacks. We take out and arrange our sleeping pads and bags, with the intention of using them for warmth and for any opportunity to lay down and rest. After getting my things organized I leave to go use the toilet tent which is set down along the edge of our group's space. To get to it is a careful climb downhill, only a few steps, but wow, the ground is not stable. It's like walking among deep piles of broken dish ware and my feet can't make purchase. I'm sliding around hoping I won't fall. I am empty of strength and energy, so navigating this goofy terrain just to use the bathroom is not fun.

Inside, I struggle for balance as the tent itself is not perfectly level. I half-straddle the seat because that's all the more space there is, while I fumble to undo several layers of clothing with numb fingers. I work to push aside clothing on my upper body in order to get to the snaps and zippers of my lower body. After I pee, reaching behind for the roll of toilet paper in its sling feels like a near impossible task. I finish up and it takes some moments to tuck things in, one layer at a time, and get zipped up again. Exhausted, I think of how I will appreciate some things differently once I'm off this mountain.

Time for lunch. Our guides have been brilliant all week with their timing, as it seems when we get to camp and are gathered in the tent for lunch, is when bad weather hits. They do it again today. Light rain started a little after we had gotten into camp and it was no big deal. Now, I just manage to sit down and the rain turns heavy like it's been switched onto high. We hear the slap of sleet and a minute later wet, sloppy snowflakes patter onto the canvas walls. Inside, it is relatively comfortable and I am relieved to be in shelter. I am cold, but not wet. With the help of hot soup and hot tea I begin to warm up.

While eating, as we watch heavy snow through the open flap of the dining tent, beyond where Tim sits, he's watching us. "Eat some more," he says, addressing several of us. It's a command, not a suggestion.

I wave a hand to dismiss the beautiful platter of food making another round, but under Tim's stern eye, I force myself to eat a little more of what's on my plate. All week, our guides have watched how we've been handling the formidable demands of the trek. Our group continues to have good (enough) vitals, we are eating (fairly) well, and doing a great (A+) job sticking to the advice of keeping hydrated. Yay, team.

Tim finishes his lunch and sets aside his plate. He says, "So let's talk about what's coming up." He shares the rest of the day's itinerary. We are to retire to our tents and meet back up at five for dinner. After dinner, he tells us, we should try to sleep a little, and then a quick snack will be served before we start out for the summit at midnight.

I lean in toward Craig, summing up our next few hours, "Rest, dinner and a little more rest." It sounds meager. We are mere hours away from our all-important summit push and I am intimidated. It's dawning on me that our day today does not have a defined ending. Sometime tomorrow, late, is when the hard work of everything will be over. It is dawning on me that our next real sleep won't be until our next camp, which will be after summiting and then getting back down onto the lower part of the mountain. It is dawning on me the anticipation of the no-sleep factor is growing into a big monster in my mind. *Yikes! What have I gotten myself into?*

I try to bring my thoughts into a more manageable perspective. I think of what's in front of me and narrow my agenda down to resting and staying warm. Craig and I return to our tent and crawl into our sleeping bags. I'm wearing tons of clothing, practically everything I'd hiked in, except my boots.

We re-group again for dinner and take turns with the oximeter. The boring little health checks are especially necessary now to flag concerns. More serious than acute mountain sickness are High Altitude Pulmonary Edema (HAPE) and High

Lower left, our campsite in Barafu. Photo by Ross.

Altitude Cerebral Edema (HACE). These conditions have to do with fluid getting into a climber's lungs or brain and can be fatal if symptoms go untreated. Our guides are equipped with supplemental oxygen, a portable hyperbaric chamber, and the expertise to discern if someone needs to turn around.

Ross asks, "How cold it will be on the summit?"

Tim shrugs his shoulders, "I don't know." He says, "Here, we just talk about temperatures in general. If it's cold or hot out." He explains that in Tanzania they don't get into specifics with the weather. Sitting and listening to Tim, I don't know if what he says is true. Is it a cultural thing, where weather isn't micro-managed and obsessed over, the way it is in the States? Or, I wonder if Tim is giving a pat answer that he gives to all his clients, not wanting to be responsible for the minutiae of the weather. Basically, what we're told is, it'll be cold.

I drink hot tea and my bottled water, and more of the hot soup Emmanuel serves. While I try to make myself eat some solid food too, Tim shares more about what we can expect and says the upcoming part of the trek isn't so much about altitude as it is about attitude. He looks directly at me while saying this. Is he talking specifically to me?

After we've eaten as much as we can, Tim asks each of us in turn what we plan to wear for our midnight appointment. He takes his time with this, looking for missing gaps that we may have and I'm sure he'll tend to any particular needs that come up. I've become fond of hand warmers while hiking in cold Colorado winters, so while Tim is going around asking about our summit clothing, I pass around a bag of hand warmers, and toe warmers too, that had been tucked away in my duffle bag all week.

Sara thanks me, "This is awesome!"

Tim dismisses us and tells us to try to rest as much as possible for the next few hours. Craig and I happily retreat to our tent. Sitting inside, yet to face our Big Moment, it occurs to me, again, we have already achieved a huge thing—the privilege of sitting up in the sky, in our tent, perched on the edge of a cliff. Huge boulders, about ten feet away, act as guard rails to keep us from falling into an abyss. Seated inside, I watch a soaring bird gliding on wind currents high above the deep valley outside, yet level with our tent. It brings contrast to the enormity of our surroundings. I am so amazed with the world.

Lots of weather had been thrown at us earlier: rain, sleet and snow. Now, it's just cold. And the altitude is affecting me. Even walking short distances around camp highlights my exhaustion. But I want to be mentally strong instead of pre-occupied by how tired I am, so I seek a tight grip on what I'm thinking about: Grit Fortitude Resolve.

I am re-organizing my backpack. "Craig, I keep thinking about survival stories I've read about and crazy things people have faced." One example is Aron Ralston who, during a canyon hike in Utah, cut off his own arm in order to escape a dislodged boulder that'd pinned him. He later wrote a book about it, which also became a movie. "Remember the movie, 127 Hours?"

"I was a little kid when we went to see that. It made me pass out." That is no joke. When our family had gone to the movie, Craig briefly fainted during a gory scene.

During this final rest period (sounds morbid) Craig and I prepare as best we can for summiting. We organize our gear with a kind of militant seriousness, sitting side by side, facing our mission, talking quietly.

"What snacks should we bring?" I hold up packets of nuts, granola bars and trail mix.

"Do you have any extra energy drink packets?" Craig gets one of his water bottles and untwists the lid.

"Will you want extra hand warmers?" I ask. I do not want my hands to get freezing cold and I offer some to Craig. "D'ya want toe warmers too?"

"Got your headlamp, Mom? Think we'll need extra batteries for them?" He asks.

"Are we good to go with water?" We both check to make sure our Nalgenes are full.

We both dress as much as possible, in order to stay warm and to minimize our efforts getting ready when the alarm goes off at 11:00. Craig isn't wearing nearly as much clothing as I am, but has a stack of items at the ready next to his sleeping bag. I have on a base layer of thin leggings under flannel-lined hiking pants, and silk sock liners under my heaviest-weight wool socks. Also, a thin tank top, and a thin long-sleeved base layer under a medium-weight flannel-blend jacket. Plus my winter jacket. Topped off with a lightweight knit hat. Next to my pillow, up against the side of the tent, my wide-brimmed hiking hat is upturned for my personal things — glasses, head-lamp, tissues and hand sanitizer. When I'm finally ready, I get all snuggled into my sleeping bag and will attempt to sleep for a few hours.

Physically, I am at rest; mentally, though, not yet. As pre-pared as we are, there is so much that's out of our hands. Like whether our bodies will continue being okay in this Extremely High altitude zone, and things like injury or the weather. I'd talked to someone who'd summited this past fall and he said it was the most miserable day of his life. My eye doctor, Dr. May, was here a few years ago, and he and his wife summited in a blizzard. Another couple I know, Fred and Susan, experienced a wildfire during their trek and somehow still managed to summit. My mind is a teeter-totter—one minute I'm confident, the next minute, not. I decide to not think too far ahead. I'm not going to worry about it.

"We're going to do well," I say to Craig, only half believing it. I want badly to be able to sleep, but again, decide not to worry about it and try to shut down thoughts that make me anxious. Instead, I think, even if I don't sleep, I am resting, and resting will count for something.

"We got this, Mom." Outwardly, Craig is James Bond calm. He's nothing but awesome and I appreciate his steadiness.

With so many people at this campsite, tents are more closely packed and Craig and I hear Swahili chatter. A handful of the crew sound so close it's as though they are right outside our tent. I'm ticked off because we are supposed to be trying to sleep and surely they know that. I have no idea what's being said, but I start to notice the rhythm of their conversation, how they seem to talk over each other, but in a jovial way, as though relaxing after a hard day's work. My annoyance fades and now I just wonder what the heck they're saying.

Back to our personal needs though, cocooned in our sleeping bags, we are desperate to get some rest. "Mom, do you know where the ear plugs are?"

I know exactly where they are. "Here you go, Hon." And I twist in a couple for myself too.

My present source of contentment: I am warm enough.

La la salaam day six, for the next four hours.

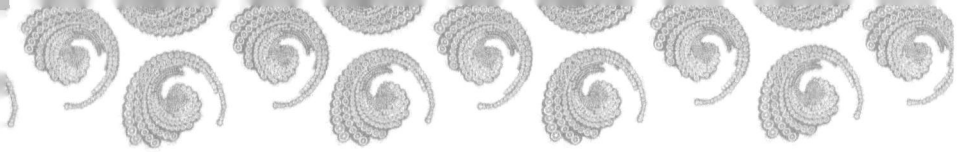

CHAPTER 13

Summer Snow

Sunday, day seven on the mountain.

Midnight marks the beginning of day seven and the beginning of our summit push. Guides Tim, Frederick and John are with us, plus Gusto. The rest of the crew will remain at Barafu. We don't have to pack up our sleeping bags or duffles because we'll be returning to this camp temporarily for a brief rest.

We trek through the entire night. Hours and hours later, deep night gradually lightens and by the time we reach Stella Point, near the tiptop of Kilimanjaro, the skies are bright and sunny.

We take a brief rest where the terrain levels out along the crater rim before moving on again. One of the guides says we have another forty-five to sixty minutes of trekking, another six hundred feet to go. On this section, as we close the gap from Stella Point to the summit, I'm calm because the physical effort is much easier on this near-flat surface. Besides the sound of my own rasping breathing, I hear the rhythmic squeak squeak of my footsteps on dry snow.

Craig takes a short video of me trekking. "I can't believe we've been out here for something like eight hours," he says, while recording. His voice is so weak I almost don't hear him.

"Huh," is all I can manage to say. I cannot even respond with a full word, I am so breathless.

We walk on, squeak on. A little after 8:00 AM we reach the summit, Uhuru Peak, at 19,341 feet.

My friend, Arnold, who I know from where I work, a place called Anthem Ranch, gave me a baseball cap, boasting "anthem Colorado!" to bring to Kilimanjaro with me. As we get ready for pictures at the spot marking the summit, I put it on so it'll be in our photos. I ask Tim to be sure to capture the logo on the hat. With this simple request, I immediately choke up — a few tears, tight throat, emotional gasp. I remember so many are pulling for us, and how important my friends and family are. There has been an outpouring of well-wishing for us among many wonderful friends back home. It's a tremendous mental boost being cheered on in this way and it's what gave me the strength I needed during the super difficult times in the middle of the night.

We pose for photos with the famous Kilimanjaro sign looming large behind us. It's a heavy wooden structure, with its topmost planks a weather-worn likeness of the Tanzanian flag, in diagonal colors of blue, green, black and yellow. Craig takes off his winter layers for a quick photo to show off his t-shirt and the name of a start-up company he's involved with. I think of how we'll always have these pictures to look back on. We are gathered in front of this sign and it feels touristy, contrived, yet our story behind these pictures reflect the tough stuff we're made of and the amazing privilege of achieving this.

Summit! From left to right: Craig (standing), Tim, me, Sara, John, Gusto (in front on the ground), Freddie, Ross (standing) and Frederick. Photo by unknown trekker.

Wonder and beauty overwhelm me. All is exquisite. During our few minutes at the top I try to take in as much of this arctic landscape as I can. Alongside the edge of the Reusch Crater, we have an easy view directly down into it. Kilimanjaro is dormant, not extinct, and ice doesn't form in the crater due to its warmth. The mountain is snow-white and the sky, bright blue, but soft pastel in places. Already, below us, clouds are bubbling up behind Mawenzi Peak. In another direction clouds are stretched out like long strands of cotton. Below us, the sun continues making its way up from the horizon. It feels strange to think we are on solid ground and at the same time seriously high up in the sky. I cannot make sense of it. On ground but in sky. Back home, the highest mountain peaks have a lot of company, surrounded in a sea of peaks. Here, other than Mawenzi, we're alone in the sky. The forever views are similar to looking out of an airplane with immense sky all around. Close up, the views in front of us are of snow and glaciers, the crater, and a scattering of other trekkers and guides.

Just snow and sky. Photo by Ross.

I feel intense joy that we did a really amazing thing and intense relief that we are about to head down. Except for heavy duty physical fatigue, Craig nor I have signs of altitude sickness and I am so grateful we are able to tolerate the extreme conditions of this place, but I'm ready to get to lower parts of the mountain. We're urged to start moving and follow in behind Frederick. His pace picks up as he leads us along the flat stretch of the crater rim. Passing up-bound trekkers, now it is our turn to cheer them on: You're Almost There! Good Job! You Can Do It!

That's me in front, with Craig next in line, alongside the Reusch Crater.
Photo by Ross.

We are back near Stella and as we approach it some of us
want to stop and rest, but we're corralled past this point. "Keep
going. Soon we will stop," the guides say. Like sheep we do as
we're told.

Kilimanjaro has six main ascent routes which converge into
three main trails up to the crater rim. On the rim is the only
area of brief two-way traffic, and now, as we drop down off
this section just beyond Stella, Frederick leads us onto one of
the only two descent trails. Because acclimatizing is no longer
relevant, these routes lack the slow, days-long switchbacks that
the up-routes do. Descending basically means going straight
down the mountain. What takes seven days to achieve summit,
will take a day and a half to go down.

With the summit behind us I imagine any challenges we've
yet to face will figuratively, and literally, be all downhill. This
upper-most part of the trail is thick with ankle-deep volcanic

ash, and as we make our way, it is like stumbling down a sand dune. Sara stumbles a lot and falls but the ash cushions her. Once, I am right behind her when she falls and reflexively grab her arm to assist her back to her feet. Only my foot has no purchase, so instead of stabilizing us, it just slides down too, leaving us both on the ground.

"Sorry, Sara!" We break out laughing.

I am breathing hard but not gasping; the effort to breathe is nowhere near what it was in the up direction. My legs, strong from days of up-hiking, are now using different muscles, and start to feel sore. A persistent thought dominates my brain— my legs hurt and want to be off this trail. But that is not an option. My practical brain says Too Bad. I'm glad for my hiking poles, a small concession, as they help take away some of the strain of down-stepping.

We trek on. Summit adrenaline circulates through me, but I'm sobered when we pass a woman in trouble. She'd fallen and is alone with a guide, crying and in pain. He pulls her up to standing and gives her hip a vigorous rub, making her cry out all the more. How badly is she hurt? How long will it take for her to get off the mountain?

Finally, Barafu Camp appears far below us. As we hike up and over the folds of mountain terrain, with each glimpse of the campsite, it becomes noticeably closer. Still, it mocks. My brain rides a euphoric high while my body is begging for rest.

At last, we approach the upslope side of Barafu and we are met by a few of the crew from our camp that have been waiting to welcome us back. They confer with our guides and inquire how we had all managed. There is lots of Swahili so I only get the gist of their conversations. I am impressed with our head guide Tim. He has endured the same physical insanities as everyone, this arctic summit climb on very little, if any, sleep, yet he is responsible for everything that goes on with our small group. Not only is he amazing for us, right now, but it blows my mind that he suffers this epic feat regularly throughout the climbing season.

Twice more we pass trekkers in distress. One woman has porters supporting her on either side. She has a foot or leg injury and is only able to bear weight on one leg. It looks like she is hurting a lot. Another time, I see a man being escorted by crew and his face is twisted in a grimace of pain. What is he suffering from?

We make it to camp, completing the three miles back to Barafu. What had taken us eight hours going up, took less than half that to return. In total, we have been trudging around for close to twelve hours. And it's only midday. We retrace our way through the sprawling camp. Walking over to our cluster of tents, we again are on crazy, unstable rocks and each step I take is wobbly and loosey-goosey. At last we reach our tent. I'm overwhelmed with relief that we've come to a complete stop.

"How's it going, Craig?" My energy meter is between zero and one.

"You know the part just below the rim?" he says. "Going down was brutal. It was like trying to ice skate down gravel for two hours." He removes his boots.

"I was thinking we were on the sand dunes of Lake Michigan." I've taken my boots off too, plus my outer shell.

"And once we were past that ashy-gravel stuff then we had to step our way over big rocks," he says. "I didn't want to twist an ankle."

"My legs were screaming," I sit down on my sleeping bag and start massaging my legs. "Especially my thighs and hips."

"My knees were on fire," he says.

However, for all the protesting joints and muscles between us, we are holding up okay and are safe back in camp. Now, we are allowed one hour of sleep, so Craig and I crawl into our bags and pass out. After what feels like a minute we are called for lunch.

I barely can eat Godlisten's delicious food and don't understand why I don't have an appetite after all the work I've done. But it's important to try to eat anyway. And while I appreciate our lunch break, it isn't all that restful because we have a full day's agenda still ahead. "There are two options for this afternoon," Tim says. "A, we go only to Millennium Camp which means a longer hike off the mountain tomorrow. B, we can push for the furthest camp down, Mweka, which means a shorter hike out tomorrow."

We highly desire the shorter, easier hike. Must be that we are in a manic, euphoric-induced mental state though, because our group defers to Tim's expertise. He knows the pros and cons. "What do you think, Tim?" someone asks. "What's your preference?"

"I think it's better to do the longer hike today," he says.

There's a mix of apprehension and resolve on our faces. Physically, this is the last thing I want to do, but I'm encouraged Tim thinks we are capable of the longer hike. What I hear him saying, in essence, is, We Are Doing Well. More specifically, as the oldest, I am—my ego is—pleased to know I'm not a hindrance to the group. Plus, a further hike today means we will sleep at 10,200 feet instead of 12,530 which is better all around for us.

"Alright, we'll go to Mweka" Tim says. "Let's be ready and meet back up in a half hour." He dismisses us.

The farther camp is a half day away with an additional five thousand foot descent. We have been on the move for over twelve hours, including our little siesta and lunch. We have been "on" since 6:00 AM Saturday. It is hard to fathom even giving thought to doing more. In our tent, we pack up for this last segment of what's been an off-the-charts adventurous day.

"Ugh, I hate hiking downhill," Craig groans.

"I hate hiking uphill," I snatch up my backpack. "I hate hiking!"

CHAPTER 14

Grueling

W e start on down. Altitude-wise, we are moving toward
a more oxygen-saturated environment, which is great.
As we go down everything will be easier—lower altitude, less
extreme weather, the promise of rest.

The guides are all business and Frederick leads us out of
camp with a sense of hurry. We are in cloud cover, rather, we
are in a cloud, and it's foggy. The trail gently descends, its slope
not challenging, but it is a slick, damp, gravelly trail and because
my legs are jelly-tired, I feel vulnerable to falling. I've been
caught off guard in the past and … BAM! down I'd go. So now,
my revised mantra is to keep walking and don't fall. Countering
my cautiousness, I'm buzzing with the exhilaration of having
just summited a tremendous huge mountain with my son. I
feel Invincible. Proud. Audacious.

Craig and I are kind of power-stepping, heavily relying on
trekking poles, and blazing away. The others lag behind, with
Ross hanging back to stay with Sara and Freddie, although he's
probably capable of trail-running. Probably capable of running
backwards, blindfolded, down this mountain. Misty fog develops

into rain and my heavy duty rain poncho easily keeps me and my backpack dry. Frederick, earlier, was using his large golf umbrella, but now has an improvised poncho protecting him and the gear on his back. Somewhere along the way, the trail becomes more steep.

It was an illusion to expect things to get easier on the way down. Today, reaching the top of Kilimanjaro, the summiting part, was the mere beginning of Very Hard Work. Some portions of our trail involve stepping down massive steps (hmm… didn't think to pack a step stool). Hour after hour of staggering down the trail, Craig and I are pretty miserable but it could be so much worse, because our feet—toes, feet, ankles—are all good to go still. People have been known to sacrifice toenails from the impact of down-stepping mile after mile. Eventually we come to the higher camp, the one we had earlier decided to pass by for the lower camp. Before the arrival of the Year 2000, the marking of a Grand New Time, Kilimanjaro National Park established Millennium Camp to accommodate an anticipated uptick in thousands of travelers. It is used both as a camp and an emergency evacuation site. What a tease it is, as we walk straight on through it. No rest for the weary.

As we hike further and further down, we are again in dense rain forest. When I am able to glance up from watching my steps, I see the trees stretching skyward and it feels like we are under the biggest-ever emerald umbrella. I hear forest music, a performance of bird sounds and rustling leaves. Giant ferns blanket any area not consumed by trees. It's magical. It's raining just slightly now; the air is full of oxygen and thick humidity coats everything wet. The trail rarely levels out and remains steep. It is wrought with rocks and tree roots and is mud-slick. My upper chest is aching from leaning so hard on my trekking poles, but I'm sure I would have to crawl on my butt if it weren't for them helping keep me upright.

Porters in thick rainforest. Photo by Ross.

Guides Tim (left) and Frederick. Photo by Ross.

We stop for a break. "Craig, can you believe it?" I find a wet rock to sit on and take off my thin gloves. "We trekked on snow this morning."

"Here, Mom," Craig hands me my water bottle from my backpack.

"And now we're in the middle of a dripping rain forest."

"What a crazy day," he sits next to me, head down and looking at the ground.

"My legs are burning." I stand back up. "I don't dare sit too long. It's too hard to get moving again when I stop."

Craig responds with a grunt. He drinks down half his water bottle.

"How ya doing, Hon?"

"I am so ready to stop," he says. He takes my water bottle and puts it back in the side pocket of my pack. He puts away my gloves for me too.

Our quick break is over and I get back on trail behind Frederick. Craig follows in behind me.

"I'm so ready to stop," he repeats. "But wouldn't trade this for anything."

"I know, me neither." For all our misery, what we're doing is no-regrets epic.

Our main crew had gone out ahead of us to set up camp at Mweka, including Gusto who'd summited with us. I'm surprised and happy when I see him, along with some others, coming up the trail to greet us. I marvel at the work of the crew and how they've helped us go up and come back down this mountain. I am so tired and yet here they are, tolerating the same conditions as us, but working and providing for our needs. I feel so grateful for them as we're gathered here on the trail. But mostly I feel a surge of relief — is this the end of today's trek?

We see many tents, tightly clustered and vying for space among towering trees, in what feels like another small village. Several other guide companies and their groups are huddled closely together, hunkered in the thick forest, under a dark gray sky. There are people everywhere; active Tanzanians and exhausted trekkers. It's only barely raining, but everything is dripping. Some leaves produce big tear drops at their tips, moisture continually pouring forth. If not for lots of other people around, this place would look like a scene out of a haunted Stephen King movie. Not that I would care, I am too tired to care. And, I pointedly deny to myself the possibility of snakes. I am sure they don't exist here.

I crave sleep. I crave to stop moving. I crave to turn off the desperate cry of my legs.

We are shown our tent and I plop into it, trying to sit down on the inside while keeping my feet outside. I take off my gaiters and muddy boots and put them under the tent's covered entrance. Craig does all these same ministrations as well but with twice the speed as me. We unpack our sleeping bags and melt into them. After a deep, zombie-like rest, we gather in the dining tent for another great meal. After eating, we stay gathered around the table, most of us nursing cups of hot tea.

Tim asks, "So, how is everyone feeling about the summit?"

Weary beyond anything, we five murmur a collective version of It Was Awesome. As we talk more about this impossibly long day, we share details about our physical aliments and mental dramas. I mention how I was nauseous part of the way and how seriously difficult it was to keep going. Someone else had

had nausea too and feared being told to turn around if they
threw up.

"It was cool," Craig says. "Walking up to the summit on
the mainly flat part from the false summit to the true one."
He's referring to the part between Stella Point and Uhuru
Peak. "And everyone coming back down is psyched for you to
be where you're at. Then when you're heading down the same
way, you're just as pumped for the people still heading up." He
reaches forward to pour more hot water for me and hands me
another tea bag.

We laugh and nod in agreement. Someone says, "Yeah, it
was fun seeing everyone cheer each other on."

Sitting around, our conversation revs up over what we'd
just done. We talk about the night sky, and how it was so
intense, how it was so dark and undiluted by city lights. Craig
says, "Being able to see the stars and constellations, and I'm
pretty sure entire galaxy clusters, while being that exposed, with
nothing around you on the side of a mountain, was insane."

Our small group sits in awe. What a fantastic and amazing
and challenging day it's been.

Craig adds, "And the sun came up, and we were higher than
the sun. Not like, the sun's on the horizon when you're driving
to work, and you're on a hill and you have to look directly at it
but, like, above the sun." We'd been able to see the curvature of
the earth and even as the sun rose, we were above it.

Lounging around Mweka Camp, I feel incredibly boosted.
We accomplished a twenty-hour day, which was tacked onto
a long day prior to this too. I am straight up ecstatic and feel
I can do anything I put my mind to. Physically, it is a thrill to
be capable of something this extreme, to be strong enough for

it. We are not yet done but we're getting through it and getting closer to the finish line.

Back in our tent I turn to Craig, "Help me do the math. We made it to Uhuru Peak, to over nineteen thousand feet, and then came down to here, around ten thousand."

"So," he says. "Since midnight, we climbed up four thousand feet, then roughly retraced those four thousand back down to Barafu."

"Yeah, for our little nap and lunch break."

He's rummaging through his duffle looking for clothes for tomorrow, "And then we came down another five thousand. Yeah, that makes it nine thousand feet altogether that we down-hiked today."

"That means a total of four up and another nine down," I say. "We did that all in one day."

"How insane is that?" Craig shakes his head.

"I am so impressed with us," I say. "What a grueling, crazy day."

My heart is big and full for doing this trip with Craig. We will always have this. I'm certain I would not have done this if it weren't for his initial interest in it. At twenty-four, he is already a hardy, experienced traveler and his easy-going attitude over-lays a passion to play hard in our big beautiful world.

"Craig, you make it so much fun to go on adventures with," I say. "We both got put to the test back there…." Earlier, we'd gotten crabby, succumbing to fatigue, protesting muscles and the difficulty of the trail. "But you still kept encouraging me the whole way."

It's around 8:00 PM. I get arranged inside my sleeping bag (sans hot water bottle) and set aside my headlamp. And now for the precious moment of closing my eyes for the night.

"Goodnight, Craig. Love you."

"Night, Mom. Love you too."

"Goodnight, last night on the mountain."

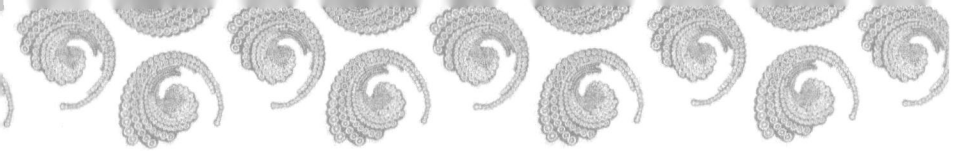

CHAPTER 15

Happy Anguish

Monday, day eight on the mountain.

Sleep was bliss. Emmanuel, for the last time, serves us morning coffee, mine, candied up just the way I like it, after a gentle tap tap on the side of our tent. Hands Craig his cup of black. Our gear and sleeping bags are heavy with moisture even though we unzipped various screen features of our tent last night for air flow. We are steeped in damp and mud is ever present.

At breakfast, our group is functioning better, with a good night's sleep apart from yesterday's exhaustion. Tim tells us we had perfect weather on the summit. Often it's very windy, or raining or snowing. Didn't think of it until he said that, but yeah, I hadn't even thought of wind during our time up there. How can you be on the highest point of the African continent, any continent, and not have wind? If we'd been hit with something crazy, like a blizzard, I doubt I would have been able to power through it. For our entire time on the mountain we have been served up with just about the best weather possible.

So many things can sabotage a summit, but here we are, blessed with good conditions. The weather has cooperated and we have managed to avoid serious problems with the altitude. No one in our group has had any major injuries or ailments. My two big toes have impressive calluses from miles of hiking in Colorado and earlier, when I'd put on clean socks for the day, I saw that I have blisters. But they're on top of my leather-tough calluses. This is the extent of wear my feet have endured.

On the way up the mountain and back down again, our head guide Tim has taken care of us trekkers with utmost professionalism. He's managed to wear a serious demeanor all week and I find it hard to read how he is feeling about it all. Is he proud of us? Are we doing okay? This is my first time on the mountain so I have no standard to go by, no way to discern how we are doing as a group. What does he think of us?

As I top off my water bottles for the day, I ask him, "Tim, how is our group doing?"

Surprised, he smiles, "I am very proud of you! You all have done a great job!" The best evidence, of course, is we all summited. Still, I wanted the affirmation.

I am in a great mood, fueled by euphoria. And, I am ready to end this trip. It's been great, now let's get it over with. I have no injuries, but my body is shutting down and I feel as though layers of physical age are being added to me all at once. My body seems to know I won't need but a little bit more out of it. Going through the simple tasks of organizing, packing my duffle and rolling up sleeping gear takes effort. Going to the toilet tent takes effort. I sigh a lot. I creep around like a frail person. I have to step gingerly over the enormous tree roots that encircle our tent, because if I stumbled I don't think I'd be able to catch myself. My normally fluid, coordinated movements have abandoned my physical self. Today, more than any other, I diverge markedly from Craig's experience. His body isn't in the downward spiral mine is.

I'm not a fan of being cold and humidity drips off everything in the forest, living and non-living things alike. I layer up, putting on light-weight leggings under lightweight hiking pants, and it looks like there is an excellent chance of rain, so I put rain pants over my hiking pants. This is three layers of pants altogether. I add my gaiters and hiking boots. My top layers include a tank top under a light weight short sleeve top, a mid-weight jacket and then my rain shell. I am prepared for cold, rainy weather.

I was not at all excited about our long trek to Mweka Camp yesterday, but it means we only face a short hike off the mountain today. We set off with John as our guide, ready to take on a mere six miles to Mweka Gate, the exit of Kilimanjaro National Park. I'm hoping for physical demands of the trail to be easier this morning, yet within five minutes I realize it is a cruel continuation of yesterday. It is still steep, muddy and awful. Again, Craig and I rely heavily on trekking poles, all in an effort to stay upright.

"John," I say. "Will you carry me?"

He erupts with a "Ha!"

I keep thinking all this hard work will end soon. But "soon" is deceptive. We keep going, down and down, following John who is practically trail-running. Like horses turned in the direction of the barn, we giddy-up hurry. We are all slipping and sliding our way down. Same as yesterday's trek — the rocks, tree roots and steep steps are covered in wet mud. I imagine it's never dry on this part of the mountain. At one point Craig does a tremendous catch after a major slip, but manages to avoid falling, and John turns around, advising, "Watch your step!"

Craig and I exchange looks that say Are You Serious? Ughh!

As it gets warmer I become aware I have too much clothing on. To remove even one layer of pants means I'd first have to remove my gaiters and boots. As we hike, we do take short rest stops along the way, but they are brief and I don't want to hold up our group for several minutes to fuss with my clothing. So I do nothing. I'm too warm. Too tired. Too sore. Waahhh!

I am focused on watching my steps and I know, as I pass through it, that I am missing seeing this splendid rainforest. It's a cool little treat though, when John draws our attention to a lone colobus monkey and we pause ever so briefly for it.

Except for yesterday's summit segment, all of the preceding days of hiking up the mountain were just slow and lovely. But hiking down, each single minute feels multiplied by twenty, as I'm unable to ignore my aching leg muscles. There are so many steep areas and my glutes and outer thighs protest so much that I can't think of anything else. My son? His face shows a fierce determination. This is not a walk in the park for him and he is fighting his own agony. He may be a little irritable but does not complain. I am so impressed.

Occasionally we pass others and I feel very snobby and almighty that we are moving faster. This is silly though. Every-one out here is doing something extraordinary. Some that we pass are going super slow (perhaps terrified of falling because of the slick mud, or possibly injured and in pain), and I admire their resilience. My thoughts bounce between wondering about what challenges other trekkers are enduring and my own little suffer-fest.

We finally come to where the trail widens and meets head
on with a dirt lane, indicating civilization must be somewhere
up ahead. The trail is no longer treacherous and it's easier to
walk, however the steep factor still exists and my legs continue
to complain. But it is better and I no longer worry about breaking an ankle or landing on my butt. There are a few little areas
alongside the road where mountain-style stretchers are parked,
ready to help get people off the mountain if needed. These rescue

Me trekking alongside John. Photo by Craig.

gurneys can tilt up and down, like a teeter-totter, and have a large fat tire centered in the middle. Seeing them reminds me how remarkable our little group has done.

Some trekkers are nearby and looking up into the trees.

"Ah! Craig, look!" We are greeted by a few blue monkeys high in the trees, opportunists looking for snacks left behind by trekkers.

"Hey, monkeys," he says, and we take a quick minute to enjoy how cute they are.

As John continues to lead us down, the road widens more. There's more activity, more people about. Wait … what are they doing?

"Craig, what's going on?" I stop abruptly and he almost runs into me. "People are just standing around, kinda like they're done hiking." As in done hiking altogether. My heart is cautiously hopeful. I think we're emerging from Kilimanjaro. I think maybe we'll stop soon.

We notice it at the same time: "Yes!" Craig and I embrace in a happy hug. (Cue tremendous cheering in my head.) You can't miss it. The Mweka Gate sign stands at a juncture where the gravel road opens up into a parking area with actual vehicles, those things that have steering wheels and tires, and where people are milling about. Mweka is one of the exit sites off the mountain and as we come closer to the sign it's like a grand invitation to reacquaint with the real world: Hey Adventurers, Welcome Back to Normal Life!

Our elevation is now 5380 feet, similar to where we live in Colorado. Since summiting yesterday morning, we have descended just shy of 14,000 feet. We approach a big construction project and John tells us new buildings for official

Kilimanjaro Park stuff are being built. We plod right through active working construction, along narrow boards atop the muddiest areas, and into a building about the size of your average convenience store.

Our boots track heavy mud up the steps and inside all over a pretty tile floor. At a counter, similar to a counter in a hotel lobby, we get in line as uniformed park officials formally register those who've come off the mountain. Our group steps forward and as we've done all week at each camp, we fill in our names and other details on a ledger. Our head guide watches as our names are then recorded on a certificate, authorized and dated by the Conservation Commissioner and the Assistant CC. When that's completed, he simply signs "Tim" in the space for Guide. I didn't know until just now that we'd receive a nice official certificate.

I turn to him "Congratulations, Tim, you got us all up there." He nods and gives me a tired smile.

Down a hall, there are real restrooms. It is a pleasure, no, it is *fantastic*, being in a modern, clean restroom with actual stalls, plumbing, and soap and water. I hold up our group for a few minutes, doing balancing exercises worthy of a gymnast, while in a stall — taking off my boots and gaiters, so that I can remove my rain pants. Then I take off my hiking pants and leggings. I put my hiking pants back on, stuff my leggings, rain pants and a couple of top layers, too, into my backpack. It takes a few more minutes to put my boots and gaiters on again. I feel so much better.

Certificates carefully packed away in our backpacks, our group leaves the Park building and we are guided past various vehicles of guide companies waiting to whisk their climbers away and off the mountain. I wonder where ours is. Turns out, none of these are for us. Foremost in my thoughts is the fact that I want to get off my feet. I want to stop walking. Yet we keep walking. We walk past a few kiosks set out along the sides of the road where drinks, snacks, and touristy items are displayed for sale. I am too tired to do more than glance their way. Unexpectedly, we step off the road and go in between some venders' set-ups, separating us from the hubbub of other trekkers and activity. This is distressing. Whaaat?! Where is Willie and the Land Rover?

We follow our guide down a narrow footpath like little ducklings in a row. I do not know what exactly we are doing. I must have missed details while changing clothes in the bathroom. I only want to know when we will stop walking. My joints have stiffened again and my whole body is worn out, drained, from all our intense hiking. Everything feels surreal and I just follow the person ahead of me. We hop-step across a little creek, but stiffness affects my coordination and I have to navigate it with care. The narrow path comes out onto a farm lane and we are led through luxuriant towering crops. After about fifteen minutes we come to an area with out-buildings and see chickens, cows, and various farm type things. I'm not paying much attention to these things, but I now understand. We have literally walked off Kilimanjaro onto another one of Simon's farms.

Our trek is over.

CHAPTER 16

Celebrate

I feel waves of relief when I see Willie's Land Rover parked near a long barn. I remember now the last time we saw him he was stranded with a bad transmission at the Lemosho trailhead and I wonder how long he had been stuck there. We go through the gate of an enclosed area where five camp chairs are set out in a lazy semi-circle. We see most of our porters and they welcome and congratulate us. Tim asks us what we want from an old refrigerator set up on the outside of a small building. Craig is handed a bottle of Kilimanjaro beer, I get a bottle of Coke. It is delicious.

Finally, we sit. WE SIT. This is not a routine, casual thing. It's a humongous reward. I have so desired to stop walking and here we are, done with walking. We are sitting. We trekkers are a worn out looking bunch, slumped in our chairs as though long since relegated to a nursing home and made to go sit in a courtyard. It is partly cloudy and a pleasant, humid seventy degrees or so. I'm glad I had stripped off layers of clothes earlier, at Mweka Gate.

A gentleman, looking out of place wearing a sports jacket and nice slacks, appears and walks toward us. He hands each of us a large envelope labeled with our names. They contain our valuables, the ones that have been locked up in SENE's office safe all week. My thick wad of cash is all here, and our passports and drivers licenses. He gives me a small flag from the Marangu Rotary Club that Simon had promised me. Forgotten until now, he also gives me the small bags of coffee I bought from our Mbahe host, Abraham. I hold a bag up to my nose and breathe in deep. Nice.

A banquet of food is being prepared. It's a performance, in a sense, as we watch the animated crew stir and chop and assemble lunch, and I presume, happily anticipating paychecks and tips. Some are looking forward to a little time off, whereas others will turn around to work another climb. Swahili chatter and laughter permeates this whole scene while we trekkers cannot muster any energy other than trying to keep our eyes open and our bodies upright in our chairs. While we wait, Ross offers to email-share photos he had taken on the mountain.

"You're amazing, Ross, thank you, thank you," I say, peeling off a bill for him from the cash in my envelope and giving him my email address. A paltry twenty bucks is all I give him.

Most of the cash I have with me is earmarked for the mountain crew who depend on tips in addition to their wages. Normally on a guided expedition, a gratuity between 10-15% of the cost of the trip is suggested. I'd written down some notes earlier, before having stepped foot in Africa, on what to tip, otherwise I'd be struggling with basic math given my current mental exhaustion. To keep things transparent and fair, SENE uses one ledger for recording tips, visible to everyone.

While we wait for lunch this ledger gets passed around; we record our names and the amount we plan to give. The money will be distributed based on a scale that reflects the crew member's work and level of responsibility, such as guides, cooks and porters. The crew is the heart and soul of this expedition and we could not have achieved this big mountain without their support. They deserve to be tipped well.

Tim gets our attention, pointing to an area nearby and says, if we'd like, we can leave hiking items or clothing we no longer want. If it's needed, SENE keeps an inventory of gear for their crew to borrow while they work a climb. Craig and I have been wearing brand new pairs of gaiters all week, but he doesn't plan to use his anymore and put them in the collection pile. Also we left some base layer tops and heavy wool socks.

Lunch is ready and we enjoy our last meal with our guides and Ross, Sara and Freddie. After eating, the porters and guides gather to sing and dance for a farewell celebration. Rather unsuccessfully, they try to engage us in their dancing. We are maybe willing to, but our limbs flop around half heartedly due to lack of energy. My son is a great dancer, but Gusto, working hard to drive up Craig's enthusiasm, is not able to make him move much beyond some foot shuffling. Still, the Tanzanian singing, whistling and clapping is cheerful and upbeat and a lot of fun to be a part of.

When the party winds down after a short while, there are collective good-byes and well-wishes between us trekkers and mountain crew. It feels abrupt. This is the last we'll see of the team who've worked so hard for us. Willie walks toward the Land Rover and signals us to follow. I am happy we had significant time to sit and rest, and because hiking is no longer a part of our itinerary, I know I can handle how the rest of our day unfolds. However, at this moment, I look forward to a major kind of resting, picturing in my mind coming to a complete stop and being sprawled out flat on my back.

Craig and Gusto. Photo by me.

Celebrate! Photo by me.

We head downslope to Moshi Town. Craig and I will begin our flights home tomorrow; the other family is going on a five-day safari. Because we don't fly out until 10:00 PM, I arranged for a one day safari not too far from the airport to give us a quick opportunity to see some African wildlife.

Before too long we arrive at the SENE office compound. Someone opens the gate in response to Willie's horn so he can enter and park. As we file out of the Land Rover, Simon is there to greet us. Naturally, he is very pleased we summited and are all doing well.

"*Jambo!* how are you?" he says, exuding big, friendly energy. "You all summited, yeah?"

There is a spattering of It Was Amazing from all of us.

We're in a sort of a group huddle, with Simon towering over everyone. "Congratulations! I'm very happy for you!" He shakes our hands. Then he says, "I'll be leading a group up in a few days." His comment strikes me — I've just done the hardest thing I've ever done in my life, but for Simon, climbing the mountain is just another hike.

I wonder aloud to Craig, "How do some people put so much living into their time on earth?"

Craig shakes his head.

Our stored luggage is brought out and loaded into the vehicle. Next thing for us is for Willie to take Craig and me to the Pink Flamingo Hotel, arranged through SENE. I'd looked at the hotel's website and it seemed nice enough, but I don't place high expectations on what it'll actually turn out to be like. I'm hoping for adequate, and coming off of several nights in a tent, I think anything at all will be adequate. Whatever the lodging, it'll be fine. We five climb into the Rover.

After a short drive from the offices, Willie turns onto a narrow gravel road and drives at a snail's pace over numerous pot holes. In just a few minutes, he parks outside of a tall gate of a fenced-in compound, and taps his horn, signaling the hotel our arrival. We unload our things, careful to set aside only the luggage that belongs to us. Ross, Sara and Freddie wait in the Rover and will be Willie's next delivery to a different hotel. Going our separate ways now, we call out to each other Good Bye and Best of Luck!

It's been a great pleasure traveling with them.

The gate is opened for us and it looks palatial inside, with a manicured lawn and a serene, beautiful building the size of a small mansion. Emotionally, I feel like a queen, in awe by the looks of this place, but physically I'm not feeling very regal. My swollen joints are causing me to move with great awkward stiffness down the gentle path leading to the front entrance. How is it possible I climbed Mount Kilimanjaro yesterday?

The large reception area has a calm feel of a wellness retreat with large windows and doorways opened up to the outdoors along the length of one side. The ceiling is several feet high with dark wood rafters, and slow ceiling fans keep the humid air moving. The day is just-right warm, not too hot, not too cold. Someone's been assigned to handle our large assortment of luggage, and after checking in, Craig and I are led to another building. Ouch, ouch, ouch... my joints are so stiff I have trouble stepping down five shallow steps through the lawn.

Craig giggles nervously, "Mom, you okay?" I grab his arm for support.

Our room is a large apartment on the lower level terrace with its own small swimming pool, steps from the door. We are situated on a hillside overlooking a sweeping valley, views stretching far out in the distance. The door is unlocked for us and we step inside. Craig drops his backpack on the floor and takes a quick survey of the place, "Sweeeet!" It feels wonderful, not just getting back to ordinary, regular things like shelter, furniture and indoor plumbing, but we have entered a place of *luxuriant*, regular things.

After Craig showers it's my turn to step in under lovely water flowing straight down on me, heavy and warm. I take my time washing away eight days worth of sweat and toil, bathing in Extreme Happiness.

Cleaned up and looking more like normal people, we make our way to the main hotel area and run into Theresa, the very nice proprietor. She asks, "Are you comfortable? Is there anything you need?" She asks what we want for dinner and launches into long detailed descriptions of all they have to offer and what do we want? I'm overwhelmed by so many choices, partly because my body and brain are functioning on a low setting, and partly because I don't really care. I am not a picky eater and I'm not craving anything in particular. I order something having to do with pasta.

Dinner is served on an immense patio adjacent to a large, gorgeous pool on the main level where we have beautiful, reaching views. Besides us, only two other tables are occupied, so it feels very private. The staff is attentive to our needs and Craig has gotten his appetite back, devouring large quantities of food. But it's strange for me, having to more or less make myself eat.

This peaceful and calm setting is helping us rebound from our little excursion. I get up and walk to the far end of the pool and from there am able to see the white crown of Mount Kilimanjaro. Craig comes over too. We stand side by side and admire the view.

It feels amazing—EUPHORIC—to have achieved climbing a very tall mountain.

I bring my arm around Craig's waist and pull him closer to me, "Wow, that was intense."

He drapes his arm over my shoulder. "We did it, Mom."

"Yes, we did."

CHAPTER 17

Balloon Strings

Tuesday, our final day in Africa.

After breakfast, served poolside on the upper patio, we do our final packing and check out. Willie arrives to pick us up and helps us load our things into the Land Rover. We have a full day to sightsee in Arusha National Park and then will be dropped off at Kilimanjaro International Airport.

Our plan includes a guided hike to see wildlife up close. Soon after we enter the National Park, we meet up with two rangers, each with high-powered rifles slung over their shoulders. They lead us to a path off the parking lot and although this hike is usually two hours, I have no desire to do that and ask for a condensed version. Straight off, as we walk past a display of mammal skeletal remains, one of the rangers starts speed-talking about a bunch of educational things about them. I try to listen and follow along, through the curtain of his accent, but my mind, still recovering from our extreme week, is not perky and alert. I immediately interrupt him and say I cannot keep up, would you please talk slower.

Soon, we see water buffalo. They are similar to bison I've seen at Yellowstone National Park, but they have interesting curved horns and a more shaggy appearance. I'm under-awed with the landscape because we've just spent a week in incredible awesomeness and this doesn't compare. But we enjoy the slow giving way of creatures we've not seen before in the wild. There are a handful of giraffes and the guides walk us close to one nibbling away at leaves on a tree. I'm nervous being so close— I've been taught to keep a respectable distance from wildlife. Apparently giraffes don't care about people presence as this one barely acknowledges us, although if it wanted, it could've reached out and kissed me on the cheek. This registers on the awe scale.

After about an hour we return to Willie in the parking lot and say good-bye to the guides. Our tour of the park continues from the backseat of the Rover. It's hot and humid, making driving around draining rather than pleasant. However, we do see a good amount of animals and it's worth the discomfort. There are numerous giraffes, baboons, buffalo. To be precise, I see a good amount of animals. Waterbuck, warthogs, pink flamingos, zebras. Craig has checked out, slouched immobile on the seat beside me, eyes closed.

When it's time for lunch, we pull into a small gravel lot and I nudge Craig out of his stupor. We follow Willie up a steep hill to a quaint gazebo with a few picnic tables, perched high on an outcropping at the edge of a lake. We unpack picnic goodies that Willie brought, and have a full-on view of the lake. Adding to the growing list of wildlife, are four hippos lounging around together in the water, their heads poking above the surface. They serenade us with their puffing and snorting all during our meal. It is *fantastic*. This registers way high on the awe scale.

In late afternoon we exit Arusha park and Willie takes us to the airport. We unload our things, tell Willie how wonderful he's been to us and part ways. Inside, we change out of our gritty safari clothes and freshen up with disposable wipes. There's not much I can do about my hair which is flat and greasy from wearing my hiking hat. We take our time over dinner while we keep an eye on the hours yet to go for our 10:00 PM flight. Finally we board and start our long travel home.

I'm mentally maxed out but get to rely on Craig getting us connected to the States in Amsterdam. We hang out near our gate.

"Mom," Craig says. "Your hair looks fine." He's exasperated. This is the umpteenth time I've asked. My hair is in dire need of washing—hat hair combined with sleeping on it during our flight. I'm sure I have a glaring cowlick on the back of my head and that I must look pretty rough. I'm facing several time zones, still, of Look Pretty Rough.

In New York, Craig gets us through complicated customs and past rude airport personnel, to our last connection.

At last, we land in Denver.

Ali is waiting for us outside of baggage claim and I give her a great big bear hug. I'm so happy to see her. She whisks us home and we arrive at our front door around 12:30 AM Thursday.

It's good to be back.

~

One week later

My body is still in recovery mode. My immune system had taken a hit on the mountain due to the high physical stress, fatigue and being cold a lot while in camp.

My lungs had undergone lots of stress too—all that heavy breathing—and I developed cold-like symptoms on our last day in Tanzania. Now it is much better, having peaked two days ago.

I am very much taking it easy physically. Getting to bed at 8:00 PM and getting up early in the morning, at 5:00 AM or so. Plus taking significant, blissful naps during the day.

A bit of diarrhea and an itchy skin rash are both resolving. Needless to say, I haven't been well enough to get back to swimming. But I have been taking easy walks, and started running again, a little.

Other than needing a few days of extra rest, Craig picks up his normal routine without effort.

Slowly, unpacking is taking place. Besides doing lots of laundry, I have meticulously cleaned up our equipment—our suitcases, backpacks, sleeping gear and duffles—before putting them away.

And, I am writing. Getting this trip written down is like using strings to hang on to balloons. This way I get to keep it, it remains a solid thing and doesn't drift off into oblivion.

One month later

News of an imminent pandemic makes headlines. Our carefully planned trip would have likely been sidelined for good were it not for Divine Timing that we went when we did.

Two months later

In the middle of March, Covid19 alters the way of life for everyone in the world. In fear of this mysterious, invisible virus, and a strong desire to avoid a fatal encounter with it, I hunker down at home. I stop going to the pool or meeting up with friends. I politely decline working from home with my part-time job. Because distractions of normal life are unavailable, it seems like a perfect opportunity to consider taking the scraps of notes about our trip and going big with it, perhaps writing a book about it. With the luxury of time on my hands, I can think of no better reason than *now* to attempt a major writing project. And this feels like the best way to share details of our experience.

Four months later

In May, Simon Mtuy started a GoFundMe campaign. He explains in his newsletter:

"The COVID-19 crisis is devastating to Tanzania tourism. Kilimanjaro guides, porters, and all crew members are most severely affected because there are no trips going and no source of income for them and their families. The Kilimanjaro Porters Assistance Project (KPAP) has asked partner companies to help out however they can. I am volunteering to go to the communities where our porters and guides live and lead small group workshops on permaculture and beekeeping so that they can learn sustainable farming methods, which have been lost to the Chagga peoples of Kilimanjaro due to modernization. This will help sustain the soil and resources of the mountain, and also help them grow food for their families and crops that they can sell in the local markets.I will be leading several workshops around the mountain to introduce these techniques, provide seeds to start their own permaculture plots, and to offer a small financial stipend to all participants to give them funds while they are not getting income from climbing trips."

Two years later

Alison climbs an academic mountain and summits with a Masters in Social Work. Way to go, Amazing Daughter.

My beautiful daughter. Selfie by Ali.

Four years later

We humans suffered through the pandemic, but our world is back in full bloom again. Distractions of everyday life are back to normal (brisk) levels and hanging on to sufficient focus to finish this book rivals the backbone needed to climb Mount Kilimanjaro itself. I'm not sure which is harder.

My daughter and son are back to their normal (sometimes hectic, sometimes stressful) lives. I'm proud of them for taking on life's challenges with grace, humor and perseverance. My hope for all of us is that there will always be a few adventures along the way.

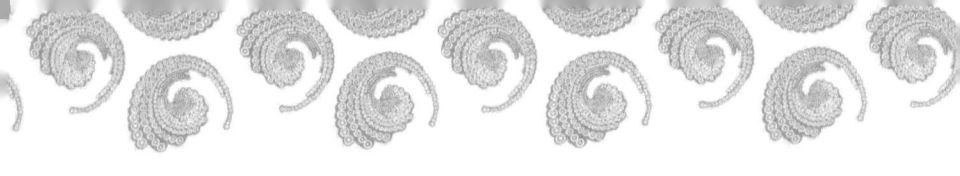

Acknowledgments

SENE

I want to thank the entire Summit Expeditions and Nomadic Experience team. From the porter assigned to toilet tent duty, to our one female porter, to Simon Mtuy at the helm of this outstanding guide company, and to everyone in-between.

Our Trekking Group

Thank you, Ross Brunner. Somehow you had additional energy to not only hike a big mountain but to take many wonderful photographs along the way. How generous of you to share them with us. It was delightful traveling with you, and Sara and Freddie. Great memories!

Anthem Ranch

Thank you to the awesome community of Anthem Ranch. So many of you have been a steady source of encouragement. Some of you were there while I prepared for the trek, some of you were there to greet me when I came back from Tanzania, and some of you are still with me, cheering me on through the years-long process of writing about it. Toward the end of my writing journey I realized that without your community the chances of completing this book would have been much lower. Your constant friendly inquiries and curiosity about my writing was enough fuel to get me there.

A few of you, previous and current residents, have made a special impact:

Wes and Rita Adams. Rita, for our hiking and trail conversations.

Kim Anderson and Carmen Valdes. For our hiking and trail conversations.

Merri and Tom Anderson. Simply, it's always good to see you at the Lodge.

Anthem Ranch after hours crew, Sandra Pinon and Delith Corral. So glad for our friendship.

Karen and Shelly Birkhold. For our hiking and trail conversations, and Yellowstone bonding.

Carol Burnett. I see you at the Lodge only on occasion, but you always have chocolate to share.

Elle and Roger Cabbage. Elle, you excel at encouraging me, not only in my writing, but in life as well. Simply, you are one of my favorite people. Roger, you and your daughter, Christina, summited Kilimanjaro years ago… hope this book brings you back there. Thanks, too, for indirectly leading me to SENE. A quick mention … thank you for your tremendous heart— please continue with the good work of your company Global Access 2030 (*ga2030.org*), which provides safe, affordable water filters to areas desperate for clean drinking water. You're an inspiration.

Nancy and Ron Campbell. Nancy, thanks for our many fun conversations. Ron, when I told you what my initial, rather long, book title was you responded with, "How about…?" Thank you, this version is better.

Judy and Paul Classen. It was cool when you'd shared the picture of when you were a young couple many years ago standing at the base of Kilimanjaro holding your six month old daughter. Paul, thank you for procuring our travel flights and insurance for Africa. Judy, thanks for being so warm-hearted.

Bonnie and David Corkum. When we first came to know each other, before Kilimanjaro, I felt safe enough to share with you a few hiking stories I'd written. And Bonnie, you'd always ask for more. Subconsciously, part of the audacity to think I could write a book and that people would want to read it, was fueled by you.

Phil and Ginny Daniels. Thanks for reading chapter one of my final manuscript and having to call me right away to tell me how much you liked it.

Joan DePuy. Many times, you gave me a listening ear as I processed my writing.

Judy and Ira Denton. Both of you are so kind, always. Ira, I hope you keep writing in some capacity — maybe a follow up to *Team Bangkok: Hearts on Ice,* the novel you wrote based on the time you and Judy spent in Thailand?

Evelyn and Gregg Dye. Gregg, for our hiking and trail conversations, and Yellowstone bonding. Evelyn, for your blunt Why Would Anyone Want to Climb Kilimanjaro You're Crazy comments.

Don Engelstad and Trudy Wood. Both of you—gentle, generous and kind.

Marge and John Fajardo. The angel pin you gave me made it to the summit. It still has a home in my backpack and is a constant trail companion. Marge, thank you for all the publishing resources you've shared.

Susan and Fred Foreman. I'm glad you'd survived that wildfire on Kilimanjaro. You had ten times the adventure I had.

Sandy and Todd Furhey. For our hiking and trail conversations.

Ben Graham. You were working in Sudan in early 2020. Sorry, I forgot to wave in your direction when Craig and I were at the top.

Midge and Glen Kane. The angel pin you gave me, that I placed inside Craig's backpack, also made it to the summit.

Rosalie and Ken Keller. Thanks, Ken, for connecting me with Howard Daniel *(howard@pen4rent.com)*, who graciously read an earlier manuscript.

Alyce and Mike Kitt. You both are awesome people. I love seeing those grandchildren dancing videos.

Betsy and John Kolber. Both of you are a constant source of encouragement. Betsy, thanks for reading my final manuscript and penning me a very sweet note about it. John, glad you liked the manuscript as well.

Jim and Alice Lafferty. You'd shared with me that your daughter, Erin, had summited Kilimanjaro years ago during the time she was in the Peace Corps in Tanzania. Sounds like she had a little more adventure than what she'd planned on—having to seek out help for her friend along the way.

Peter Lamb. For our hiking and trail conversations, and Yellowstone bonding. You'd thanked me for firing up your desire to get back outside. Rest in Peace, Pete.

Penny Landuyt. Penny, thanks for being one of my early Readers.

Judy and Larry Oehler. Thanks for your curiosity, about my adventures and my writing.

Omar Mainero. Thanks for our writing conversations and letting me introduce you to the Adult Writing Group at the Broomfield library. I wish you all the best with your big project.

Deb O'Neill and Karen Musick. You are among my favorite swimmer friends. Deb, thanks for reading my final manuscript and your thoughtful comments.

Laurie and Linc Nesheim. Laurie, you and sweet Linen were so kind to listen as I read my final manuscript to you. I aways look forward to seeing you and Linc and Linen at the Lodge.

Jean McArthur and Ed Orlosky. Jean, thanks for being one of my early Readers. Wish you both were still at Anthem.

Gayle and Randy Preheim. Always wonderful to see you at the Lodge. Gayle, again, thanks for the ice cream treat one evening during a concert at Anthem.

Chris and Joe Roarty. You both are amazing. Chris, thank you for reading my final manuscript and helping with last minute tweaks.

Karyn and Richard Schad. Richard, you wrote *The Taste of Air: LAM: A Love Story.* Your book holds a special place in my heart for how your love for each other was shaped by immense health challenges. Your story highlights that each and every breath we take is a gift.

Dorothy Schaefer. I may not see you often at the Lodge, but you never fail to ask how my book is coming along.

Carol and Ivan Schaefer. Thanks for your interest in my adventures.

Marcia and Arnold Sorocki. My summit photos look so dorky because you gave me the "anthem Colorado!" hat. I kept tilting my face down so the words on hat would be seen.

Sheila and Pat Talbot. Pat, you are a prolific writer having published several books, including *Expose: Dangers of Residential Fracking - A Comprehensive Risk Analysis.* Thanks for being a constant support of my writing and for being one of my early Readers. Sheila, I appreciate your friendly smile whenever I see you, which isn't often enough.

Anthem Ranch Work Colleagues

Thank you to my work colleagues, current and previous. Some of you in particular have endured the gauntlet of my slow, sometimes dramatic issues with my writing. You have been so patient.

Summer Asbury. Thankful for our friendship. You are an amazing young woman, and I hope you and your husband, Matt, never stop exploring.

Robyn Biggers. Your faith in me evident when you gave me a Christmas gift two years ago, a customized mug engraved "Future Best Selling Author." Couldn't ask for a better supervisor.

Taylor Downs. You read my final manuscript and said it was "riveting," causing a significant endorphin rush to my brain. And you caught those sneaky little typos that no one else did. veni vidi vici

Katherine Erstad. You helped me present Kilimanjaro to Anthem Ranch via Zoom during early Covid times when no one was allowed to gather in groups. And, always, you're an encourager.

Derek Frost. You're my honorary writer-therapist, many times giving me space to vent frustrations over minutiae of my writing process.

Runoda Larsen. Glad for our friendship. You are Scheduler-Extraordinaire at Anthem and are essential for keeping things running smoothly at the front desk; smartest of the bunch.

Lee Ann Longnecker. Glad for our friendship, at work and outside of work. Maybe a significant hike is in our future if we can manage to get time off at the same time. Let's go!

Adult Writing Group of the Broomfield Library

I appreciate our whole group, those who've been there from the start and those who may come for a visit just once. Helps make learning the craft of writing less painful and more fun. To all of you, I want to share this Richard Bach quote, "A professional writer is an amateur who didn't quit."

Erin Dees. Erin, if you're reading this, I know you have important stories to tell. I will be waiting for them.

John Matthews. Thanks for reading my final manuscript. I had to make a slight adjustment to it when you informed me there are no tigers in Africa. Lions, yes. Tigers, no.

David Taylor. You're funny, humble and smart. You're a great leader for our writers group although you deny this and refer to yourself as "the guy who sends out the emails."

Lois Vanderkooi. Glad for our friendship and getting to meet over coffee once in a while. All the best with your writing and your book.

Greg Weber. Good to see you on those third Wednesdays of the month. Thanks for inviting your friend, children's author, Sonja Wendt, to one of our meetings. I learned some things about publishing and used one of her resources for my book designer.

Nuts and Bolts Support

Sarah Chauncey, my book editor. Sarah, you'd suggested I take my stale trek narrative and put more of Me on the page. This prompted months of blowing up my story into memoir. My book became something entirely different, a survivor's story from having been brought up in a home where disappointment rather than love was the predominant feature. Although the memoir form was cathartic to write, I brought the story all back down to my original intent—which was to share my trek. I did however bring my two kids more into the mix and the stepladder progression of active travels we did. Thank you for your wisdom.

Daring Girls. After I returned from Africa I sought out how to make a positive contribution in some way to the friendly people of Tanzania. I found Daring Girls *(www.DaringGirls.org),* previously known as Africaid, a program that builds up the lives of girls and young women. Their site states, "Building on more than a decade of designing, localizing, and supporting mentoring programs with our flagship partner in Tanzania, Daring Girls supports UNESCO Award Winning girls' mento-ring programming designed to help girls succeed in their edu-cation, and in life. We support needs as they are defined by our local partners who live and work in the communities they serve. The programs we support were designed with the involvement of adolescent girls, their peers, families and wider communities to ensure stakeholder participation."

Rebecca Finkel. My book designer (*www.FPGD.com*). So glad I found you through a connection at my library writing group. Inside and out, the book is gorgeous, thanks to your talent with design. You also have been a tremendous help with my website. I appreciate your patience and hand-holding.

Patrick Hartig. Thanks for the adventure on the seriously long loop hike in Rocky Mountain National Park in 2017. We did twenty miles on day one, zero on day two while we relaxed in Grand Lake, and finished the last eighteen miles on day three. Although I was thoroughly worn out, this gave me a hint of what my body was capable of.

Mike Jackoboice. Thanks for being one of my early Readers. And, as 1977 high school class president, you encouraged me to attend our fortieth reunion, which terrified me, as high school hadn't been a good experience. Thanks for the push. And, congratulations on your editing work on the recently published *A Trial of Innocents* by Michael Swiger.

Paul and Gladys Klassen. You have given much. You'd entered into my life at a joyful but difficult time, when I was thirty two years old and entering mom-hood. You mentored me and led me to church, to Christ. Paul, we'd met while doing laps at the Y in Edmond, Oklahoma while I was heavy pregnant with Alison. Four years later, you baptized me in that same swimming pool, this time, when I was pregnant with Craig. I was—am— blessed by the love you both showed me.

Jennifer Lusk. It's always good getting together for walks or meeting up over coffee. Many times you've helped me process life, and by extension, the writing of my book. Nice to have a therapist friend. And, although we don't swim together, thanks for striking up a random conversation at the Broomfield pool three years ago.

Nancy Patterson. We've been hiking partners for six years (wow!) because you tolerate getting up before dawn to get to the trailhead early. Thanks for being a steady source of wisdom in my life.

Antonia Williams-Gary. We met at the weekly Writers Workshop in Dallas-Fort Worth over ten years ago. You became a role model for me, as I watched your journey of writing and publishing your memoir, *Reclaimed.*

Alison and Craig! I'm crazy thankful for you—it would take an entire book to express how much you mean to me. Also I want to recognize your dad, James. And James' sister and brother in law, Helen and Roger Nooner, along with their two adult kids, Natalie and Christopher. And soon-to-be Chris' wife, Sierra. You all are the best family I ever had.

Best adventure of my life—my kids.

About the Author

Kerry McGlynn likes to play and explore outdoors. She hikes often; her favorite trails are in Rocky Mountain National Park. She enjoys skiing in the winter, and kayaking or canoeing in the summer. Once in a while, she attempts adventure way beyond reasonable comfort. Visit her website at *www.KerryMcGlynn.com.*

www.ingramcontent.com/pod-product-compliance
Lightning Source LLC
Chambersburg PA
CBHW020452130626
46549CB00001B/397